WILLS FROM

LATE MEDIEVAL VENETIAN CRETE

1312–1420

3

WILLS FROM

LATE MEDIEVAL VENETIAN CRETE

1312–1420

Volume 3

Sally McKee
Editor

Dumbarton Oaks Research Library and Collection

Washington, D.C.

Library of Congress Cataloging-in-Publication Data

Wills from late medieval Venetian Crete, 1312–1420 / Sally McKee, editor.
    p.   cm.
    Includes bibliographical references and index.
    ISBN 0–88402–245–5 (alk. paper)
    1. Wills—Crete. 2. Crete—Genealogy. 3. Crete (Greece)—History—Venetian rule,
1204–1669—Sources. I. McKee, Sally.
CS737.C74W55 1998   97–42311
929′.34959—DC21   CIP

Contents

Volume 3

List of Testators

1. Fenga, wife of Bartholomeus Curtalo, 4 January 1317/18.
2. Georgius de la Rota, 14 September 1320.
3. Sophia, wife of Nicolaus Colona, 21 May 1319.
4. Gulielma de Milano, 22 October 1320.
5. Maria, daughter of the late Philipus Quirino, 4 May 1321.
6. Marcus Capaci, *caligarius*, 31 May 1321.
7. Maria, wife of Marcus Franco, *murarius*, 2 October 1322.
8. Franciscus Dadho, 6 March 1318.
9. Thodhoti, wife of Antonius Castamoniti, 23 June 1323.
10. Potha, wife of Nicolaus Cauco, 28 November 1323.
11. Seni, daughter of Nicolaus Cerca, wife of Petrus Brunelo of Stimpalia, *hab. Stimpalia,* 8 February 1323/24.
12. Thomasina, widow of Petrus Sclença, 10 July 1324.
13. Philipa, wife of Iohannes Barbadico, 18 May 1324.
14. Cali, daughter of Nicolaus de Riço, wife of Hemanuel Habramo, *aurifex*, 3 September 1324.
15. *Frater* Iohannes, son of the late Nicolaus Iustiniano, 20 October 1329.
16. Anastassu, widow of Nicolaus Caravello, 30 July 1328.
17. Maria, daughter of the late Iulianus Vassalo, wife of Petrus Mudacio, son of Iacobus Mudacio, 15 February 1329/30.
18. Auracha, *iudeus*, son of the late Sambatheus Chomati, *iudeus*, 13 March 1330.
19. Philipa, daughter of the late Leonardus Habramo, wife of Petrus Quirino, son of Nicolaus Quirino, 9 December 1329.
20. Iacobus Cordeferro, 15 November 1330.
21. Franciscus Goço, *notarius*, 26 April 1341.
22. Pliti, widow of Leo Cavatorta, 13 May 1327.
23. Petrus Mudacio called Parlatus, 21 March 1325.
24. Leo Cofina, *fornarius*, 30 June 1346.
25. Aniça Rosso, widow of Nicolaus Rosso, 20 August 1346.
26. Marçoli Bollani, wife of Iacobus Bollani, 24 September 1346.
27. Hellena Bono, 27 October 1346.
28. Antonius Pilliça, *piscator*, 2 March 1346.
29. Cali Agapito, widow of Andreas Agapito, 29 August 1347.
30. Costas Pefani, 24 August 1347.
31. Caladia, widow of Raphael Romello, 28 May 1348.
32. Sophia, wife of Hemanuel Saxo, 30 November 1347.
33. Marchesina, widow of Paganucius, *spatarius*, 3 January 1347/48.
34. Massimus de Rimano, 30 January 1347/48.
35. Nicolota, widow of Nicolaus Naptopulo, 7 February 1347/48.
36. Petrus de Armin, 27 February 1347/48.
37. Maria, wife of Nicolaus Brexiano, *notarius*, 22 February 1347/48.
38. Herini Venerio, widow of Marcus Venerio, 16 March 1348.

39. Aniça, wife of Antonius Cirita, *caligarius*, 22 March 1348.
40. Theodora, wife of Vassilus Suriano, 20 March 1348.
41. Hemanuel Lathura, 23 March 1348.
42. Herigina, wife of ser Nicolaus Piçamano of Venice, 30 March 1348.
43. Paulus Quirino, son of the late *nobilis vir* Hemanuel Quirino, 23 January 1347/48.
44. Georgius Mussalo, 11 April 1348.
45. Nicolaus Plachina, 12 April 1348.
46. Catarina de Molino, wife of ser Facinus de Molino of Venice, 13 April 1348.
47. Hellena, wife of Iohannes de Spoliti, 19 March 1348/49.
48. Antonius de Firmo, 12 April 1348.
49. Georgius de Filaretis, *notarius*, 27 March 1348.
50. Nichiforus Paulopulo, 16 April 1348.
51. Petrus de Rubeis of Padua, 17 April 1348.
52. Simeo Greco, 26 March 1348.
53. Hemanuel Paulo, son of the late Petrus Paulo, *faber*, 7 February 1347/48.
54. Iohannes Iallina, son of the late ser Michael Ialina, 19 April 1348.
55. Agnes Paradiso, wife of ser Simonetus Paradiso of Venice, 20 April 1348.
56. Marçoli, wife of ser Andreas Iustiniano of Venice, 18 April 1348.
57. Antonia Quirino, daughter of the late ser Antonius Quirino, 18 April 1348.
58. Hemanuel Rosso, son of ser Petrus Rosso, 17 April 1348.
59. Apostolli Damiano, *sutor*, 10 April 1348.
60. Vasili Crasudhi, 31 March 1348.
61. Marcus de Firmo, *murarius*, 16 March 1348.
62. Marinus Mauroceno, *aurifex*, 19 April 1348.
63. Mariçoli, widow of ser Marcus Corario, 24 April 1348.
64. Marinus Quirino, son of the late *dominus* Nicolaus called Turin of Venice, 3 May 1348.
65. Balducius de Rimano, 20 April 1348.
66. Thomas Quirino, 8 May 1348.
67. Iohannes Popo, son of the late Dominicus Popo, 25 May 1348.
68. Potha, widow of Hemanuel Dandulo called Patermo, 13 April 1348.
69. Marchesina Popo, widow of Dominicus Popo, 1 June 1348.
70. Maria Gradonico, widow of ser Michael Gradonico, 20 June 1348.
71. Felix Bono, 18 March 1348.
72. Hellena de Millano, widow of Phylippus de Millano, 28 June 1348.
73. Mabilia, daughter of the late Thomas Moço, 14 June 1348.
74. Simon de Torcello, 12 April 1348.
75. Antonius Belli, 23 June 1348.
76. Thomasina, wife of Iohannes Bono, 3 April 1348.
77. Nichitaria Petaço, widow of Thomas Petaço, 28 December 1346.
78. Thomas Bollani, son of the late ser Nicolaus Bollani, 22 April 1348.
79. Iohannes Venetando, 15 September 1346.
80. Catarina, wife of Blasius Blasii de Riva, 24 April 1348.
81. Paulus Corario, son of the late ser Phylippus Corario, 27 June 1348.
82. Cali, wife of Constantinus Vlasto, *hab. in casali Pigi*, 22 April 1349.
83. Hellena, widow of Nicolaus Habramo, son of the late Antonius, 3 September 1350.

84. Maria Cornario called Costicena, widow of Antonius Cornario, *murarius*, 7 January 1337/38.
85. Herini, widow of Nicolaus [...], 14 October 1369.
86. Theodorus Mercato, 6 June 1372.
87. Georgius de Molino, son of the late ser Marcus, 10 November 1370.
88. Nicoleta Marcello, wife of Georgius Marcello, 19 October 1372.
89. Antonius de Mediolano, *stipendiarius pedester*, 31 March 1373.
90. Hemanuel Torcello, called Bonfadio, *hab. casalis Ambronorum*, 21 April 1373.
91. Dimitrius Theologiti, *cerdo*, 30 July 1372.
92. Facius de Risticho, 9 July 1373.
93. Vasilius Carasa, 6 February 1371/72.
94. Cali, daughter of Samuel Nomico, *iudea*, 18 June 1373.
95. Andriola de Carra, 25 November 1370.
96. Nicolaus Maçamurdi, 25 November 1370.
97. Chaluda Balbi, *iudea*, no date.
98. Nicolaus Sclavo called Vagiano, 25 September 1374.
99. Bonacursius Brancha of Mantoa, *caporalis pedester*, 31 October 1374.
100. Dimitrius Catellan, 20 August 1374.
101. Theodorus Franco, *hab. in casali Selopulo*, [...] November 1374.
102. Herini, wife of Moscoleus Selopulo, *hab. in casali Ambrusia*, 23 February 1320/21.
103. Antonius de le Done, *piliparius*, 30 April 1339.
104. Marcarius, *monachus de Troia*, 24 March 1332.
105. Herini, widow of Nicolaus Fosculo, 6 May 1332.
106. Catafigi, *monacha, que vocabar* Cali de ca' Quirino, 27 July 1333.
107. Iohannes Saracenus, 6 June, no year.
108. Eudhochia, *iudea*, wife of Rabi Peres, *iudeus*, no date.
109. Helea, *iudea*, wife of Salomon Curtesi, *iudeus*, 29 September 1333.
110. Marchesina, wife of Nicolaus Alberto, *preco*, no date.
111. Paulus Chrusoveloni, *hab. in casali Sancti Blasii*, 18 July 1334.
112. Iohannes Trivixano, 28 July 1334.
113. Tomasinus Trivixano, no date.
114. Cali de Mothono, 13 April 1335.
115. Helena, wife of Iohannes Pantaleo, 6 September 1335.
116. Michael Vataci, 30 September 1335.
117. Maria, wife of Nicolaus Brexano, 8 November 1335.
118. Ubertas, widow of Bartholomeus de Milano, 28 April 1335.
119. Iohannes de Milano, *murarius*, 26 January 1335/36.
120. Marcus Fradhelo, son of the late Iohannes Fradhelo, 16 March 1335.
121. Eudhochia, *iudea*, widow of Iacobus Blancula, *iudeus*, 26 February 1335/36.
122. Michael Suriano, 23 May 1336.
123. Iohannes de Rugerio, son of the late Hemanuel de Rugerio, 26 July 1336.
124. Henrigina, wife of Iohannes Balduvino, 23 September 1336.
125. Iacobina, wife of Nicolaus Habramo, 28 March 1336.
126. Hemanuel Sacreto, 1336.
127. Catherina, widow of Antonius Calbo, 30 May 1336.

128. Caterina, widow of Paulus de Stella, 14 January 1336/37.

129. Felix, wife of Petrus Petraca, *murarius*, of Venice, 26 February 1336.

130. Porfira, *iudea*, wife of Helia Verioti, *iudeus*, called Papu, 17 September 1335.

131. Maria, widow of Georgius Paramandi, 8 October 1339.

132. Caliça, wife of Marcus Raguseo, 5 February 1339/40.

133. Mariçoli, wife of Iohannes de Canale, 8 February 1339/40.

134. Esther, *iudea*, wife of Lingiachus, *iudeus*, son of Salachaya, *sacerdos*, 7 June 1340.

135. Marinus Gisi, son of the late *dominus* Robertus Gisi, 17 February 1383/84.

136. Eudochia, wife of Vaxilius Suriano, 22 March 1332.

137. Eudochia, *iudea*, widow of Pothas, *iudeus*, 12 October 1340.

138. Petrus Remerius of Venice, 8 January 1340/41.

139. Helena, widow of Matheus Aliurando, 29 February 1340/41.

140. Agnes, wife of Nicolaus Taiapetra, *notarius*, 15 January 1338/39.

141. Marchesina, wife of Litofredus Symeon, 27 May 1341.

142. Soi, *iudea*, wife of Chavi, *iudeus*, 10 May 1341.

143. Calinichi Samea, *monacha*, 6 August 1341.

144. Marchesina, widow of Nicolaus Habramo, 15 January 1339/40.

145. Alba, wife of Raphael Baxilio, 24 February 1340/41.

146. Angelota, widow of Nicolaus Gradonico, 21 February 1345/46.

147. Cecilia, widow of Federicus de Ragusio, 27 August 1346.

148. Petrus Valaresso, 30 April 1335.

149. Maria, widow of Leo Calergi, 2 November 1346.

150. Leo Sanuto of Venice, 20 March 1347.

151. Martha, *monacha, vocata in habitu layco* Maria Chyriacopulina, formerly *hab. in casali Furfura,* 29 April 1347.

152. Eugenia Cornario, *monacha*, 3 April 1342.

153. Çaneta, wife of Bartholomeus de Rippa, 18 July 1344.

154. Nicolota, widow of Bartholomeus Venerio, 29 December 1345.

155. Calo Suriano, 17 June 1347.

156. Agnes Milumercena, 4 February 1346/47.

157. *Papas* Georgius Coroni called Chrussolura, 7 January 1347/48.

158. Cherana, wife of Helia Belança, *iudeus*, 26 November 1342.

159. Nicolaus Dandulo called Belinus, 20 May 1351.

160. Fradela, widow of Albertinus Cornario, 11 January 1341/42.

161. Michael de Despotato, 26 September 1354.

162. Phylippus Maçamano, 30 March 1354.

163. Herini, daughter of the late ser Hemanuel Ialina, wife of Theodorus Gemisto, *medicus* of Constantinople, 12 December 1358.

164. Daniel Gastrea, *ieromonachus*, 27 March 1359.

165. Nicolota, widow of ser Petrus de Vigoncia, 4 November 1357.

166. Cali, widow of Iohannes Tataro, *marangonus*, 1 June 1359.

167. Georgius Liveri, *corrigiarius*, 18 October 1359.

168. Cali, former wife of Georgius Perdicari, now *monacha et pro habitu monachali vocata* Cassiana, 15 April 1358.

169. Helea, *iudea*, wife of Alcana Politi, *iudeus*, 20 November 1347.

170. Iohannes Bevardo, *hab. casalis Laguta*, 30 August 1352.
171. Helena, wife of Angelus de Vano, 14 June 1352.
172. Nicolaus Marçangelo, 24 May 1357.
173. Phylippa, widow of Iohannes Staurachi, 13 November 1357.
174. Constantinus Cafato, *hab. casalis Boni*, 30 August 1353.
175. Elena, widow of ser Petrus Mudacio, 23 January 1359/60.
176. Thomasina, wife of ser Thomas Advonale, 8 March 1348.
177. Iohannes Yesse, *hab. in casali* [...], 4 November 1361.
178. Iohannes Ialina, 22 May 1353.
179. Agnes Sclavo, 22 January 1347/48.
180. Phylippa, widow of Petrus Sancti, 27 August 1348.
181. Thomasina, wife of Nicolaus Matono, 17 May 1351.
182. Benedicta, widow of Dominicus Gradonico, 26 July 1351.
183. Nicolaus Venerio *maior*, 17 October 1351.
184. Xeni Mauroianena, widow of Marcus Rapani, *hab. in monasterio Dei Genitricis de Dhiavatina*, 6 September 1335.
185. Hemanuel Vergici, 18 February 1342/43.
186. Cherana, wife of Nicolaus Corfioti, *hab. in casali Bassia*, 10 January 1351/52.
187. Georgius Rosso, *aurifex*, 12 January 1351/52.
188. Beata, wife of ser Georgius de Canale, 2 April 1352.
189. Sophya, widow of *papas* Georgius Pendamati, 18 May 1352.
190. Theodorus Çavardalino, *filius divisus* of Nicolaus Çavardalino, 31 December 1351.
191. Cali, *iudea*, wife of Lingiachus Pastela, 19 October 1341.
192. Dardius Balbi, *filius divisus* of ser Petrus Balbi, 12 July 1352.
193. Marula, wife of Michael Ialina, *butiglarius*, 12 July 1352.
194. Agnes, widow of ser Marcus Contareno, 16 June 1345.
195. Nicolaus de Cremona, June 1343.
196. Herini, daughter of the late Georgius Vestarchi, widow of Nicolaus Triandafilo, 29 December 1347.
197. Phylippus Çane, son of the late *dominus* Nicolaus Çane called Pançono, *de confinio Sancte Marie Matris Domini de Venetiis*, 31 March 1348.
198. Mariçoli, wife of Nicolaus Pantaleo, 2 [...] 1348.
199. Iacobina, widow of Angelus Teocari, 1 June 1346.
200. Mariçoli, daughter of ser Andreas Pantaleo, 24 March 1348.
201. Leonardus de Molino, [...] April 1348.
202. Malgarita, widow of ser Romeus Faletro, 23 December 1344.
203. Benvenuta Trivisana, 15 February 1347/48.
204. Claretus Foscareno, 26 April 1348.
205. [...] Cornario, son of the late *dominus* Andreas Cornario of Venice, 30 April 134?.
206. Iohannes Cauco, son of the late Marcus Cauco, 13 September 1347.
207. Helena, wife of Iohannes Capuço, *hab. in casali Polemissa*, 29 August 1348.
208. Contessa, wife of Paulus de Rugerio, 1339.
209. Iacobus Cornario, son of the late ser Iacobus Cornario, 25 February 1348/49.
210. *Presbyter* Marcus Cavalcante, 15 April 1349.
211. Catherina, widow of the late *nobilis vir* Nicolaus Michael of Venice, 15 July 1349.

212. Helena, widow of Marcus Maçamurdi, 17 July 1348.
213. Nicolaus Mercato, 2 January 1349/50.
214. Magdalena, *monacha, in habitu laico vocabar* Maria, widow of Iohannes Afrato, 12 February 1349/50.
215. Potha, *iudea*, wife of Laçarus, *iudeus*, 15 May 1350.
216. Gregorius Langadhioti, 12 June 1350.
217. Maria, *raptrea*, 30 May 1350.
218. Daniel Greco, 7 May 1348.
219. Marcus de Canale, 6 May 1348.
220. Thomasina, widow of Iacobus Cornario, 23 March 1348.
221. Antonius Secreto, son of the late *dominus* Iohannes Secreto, 21 May 1348.
222. Petrus Çampani, son of the late ser Iohannes Çampani, 31 May 1348.
223. Phylippus de Rippa, *filius divisus* of ser Bartholomeus de Rippa, 2 August 1347/48.
224. Helena, widow of Chyrilus Pantaleo, 6 May 1348.
225. Paulus Quirino, 9 June 1348.
226. *Papas* Vaxilius Chrusolura, 11 April 1345.
227. Anastasu, *iudea*, wife of Iaco, *iudeus*, son of the late Sapiens, 10 December 1336.
228. Nicolaus Habramo, son of the late ser Marinus Habramo, 6 August 1353.
229. Theotochius Egripioti, 3 August 1352.
230. Maria, wife of Georgius Selopulo, *aurifex*, 20 March 1345.
231. Antonius Chandachyti, *filius indivisus* of Michael Chandachyti, *arcerius*, 16 July 1361.
232. Constantia, widow of ser Angelus Quirino, 17 May 1359.
233. Potha, wife of Michael Pisano, 30 May 1358.
234. Helena, wife of Dominicus Geno, 29 October 1338.
235. Iohannes Alimanus, 21 February 1328/29.
236. Theodosius Armachi, 18 January 1325/26.
237. Afrati, wife of Micali Clomidhi, 2 April 1327.
238. Iohannes Cornario called Sclavinus, 7 March 1319.
239. Marcus Cornario *de domo maiori*, 30 August 1326.
240. Agnes, wife of Hemanuel Gavala, 6 June 1322.
241. Hemanuel Gavala, 7 April 1328.
242. Bonuça, wife of Philippus Gisi, 4 May 1318.
243. Agustinus Gradonico, 4 October 1328.
244. Marçoli, wife of Iohannes Greculo, 17 February 1328/29.
245. Georgius Lumbardo, 25 November 1327.
246. Kali Milea, 24 October 1325.
247. Marchesina, daughter of the late Thomas Morari, 22 May 1327.
248. Marchesina, widow of Nicolaus de Plasencia, *aurifex*, 27 August 1329.
249. Plecti, *iudea*, 25 August 1327.
250. Raphael Romano, *sartor*, 23 July 1328.
251. Tomasina Sclença, 21 August 1324.
252. Costantinus Selopulo, 25 April 1325.
253. Helena Vaxallo, widow of Iulianus Vaxallo, 6 April 1319.
254. Georgius Vordali, *hab. in casali Vuchu*, 19 August 1327.
255. Frangulla Catellano, wife of Andreas Catellano, 22 December 1350.

256. Marçoli, wife of ser Andreas Cornario, son of *dominus* Alexius Cornario *de domo maiore*, 31 August 1351.
257. Andreas Quirino of Venice, son of the late *dominus* Bertucius, 8 October 1364.
258. *Nobilis vir* Marinus Contareno of Venice, called Barbadusia, 5 March 1348.
259. Phylippa, daughter of the late Marcus Mudacio, wife of Iohannes de Grimaldo, 30 May 1348.
260. Ser Marinus Venerio, son of the late Blasius, *de contrata Sancte Thodorie*, [...] 1361.
261. Iohanninus Cornario, son of *dominus* Marcus, 3 June 1362.
262. *Papas* Bartholomeus de Corintho, *monachus*, 22 June 1360.
263. Marcus Brogognono, son of the late *dominus* Petrus, 12 July 1360.
264. Agnes, widow of *dominus* Iacobus Gradonico, 18 October 1360.
265. Nicolaus Ragusio, 22 June 1362.
266. Marchesina de Canale, widow of ser Marinus de Canale, 25 August 1362.
267. Iohannes Murisco, *marinarius*, 26 July 1352.
268. *Frater* Petrus de Filaretis of the Order of *Fratres Minores*, son of the late Georgius de Filaretis, 2 September 1362.
269. Herini, *diaconissa, calogrea*, 8 September 1362.
270. Nicolaus Gisi, son of the late *dominus* Robertus Gisi, 28 June 1361.
271. Petrus Taliapetra Buali, 1 December 1362.
272. Michaletus Mauroceno, son of the late *dominus* Franciscus of Venice, 10 April 1363.
273. Pantalucius Quirino, son of the late Leonardus, 15 June 1362.
274. Ser Belellus Nani of Venice, 25 February 1362.
275. Andreas Cornario, son of *dominus* Alexius Cornario *de domo maiori*, 19 June 1360.
276. Laurentius Quirino, son of the late *dominus* Nicolaus, 16 June 1362.
277. Nicoletus Cornario, son of the late *dominus* Iohannes of Venice, 29 April 1362?.
278. Antonius Mudacio, son of the late *dominus* Petrus, 22 December 1370.
279. Maria Quirino, widow of Leonardus Quirino, 10 January 1351/52.
280. Franciscus Caravello, son of the late *dominus* Marcus, 22 August 1371.
281. Katerina Beligno, daughter of the late Ognebene Beligno, 14 August 1352.
282. Nicolaus Gradonico, *mensurator*, called Muglo, 8 July 1352.
283. Theologu, wife of Iohannes Gradonico, *preco*, 13 July 1350.
284. Tomaxina, widow of Petrus Rosso, 13 August 1350.
285. Iohannes de Vigla, 25 October 1355.
286. Laurencius Manolesso, son of the late ser Andreas, *de confinio Sancti Barnabe de Venetiis*, 22 August 1366.
287. Maria, wife of Laurentius Çate, 9 April 1363.
288. Marula, daughter of the late Nicolaus Gavra, 31 March 1363.
289. Philippa, daughter of the late Vasilius Iustiniano, widow of Georgius de Ponte, 19 January 1351.
290. Sofia Gulyaçena, 12 October 1363.
291. Alisse, daughter of Iohannes Cherchioli, wife of Marcus de la Turre, 7 January 1363/64.
292. Andreas Iustiniano of Venice, son of the late *dominus* Marcus Iustiniano, 9 May 1359.
293. Costas Monomato, 8 January 1363/64.
294. Iohaninus Geno of Venice, son of the late *dominus* Dragonus Geno, 15 July 1364.
295. Dimitrius Paneromitti, 7 December 1357.

296. Iohannes Dandullo, son of the late ser Belinus Dandullo, 17 September 1362.

297. Grafeus Saxo, *in charçere dominationis detemptus*, 4 July 1364.

298. Bartholameus Abramo, son of the late Vitalis Abramo, *de Castro Bonafacii*, 25 December 1364.

299. Iacobus, son of the late Iohannes Burin *de Bononia, speciarius*, 23 March 1365.

300. Beata, daughter of the late ser Marinus de Molino, wife of Dominicus Quirino, 9 May 1365.

301. Dominicus Quirino, son of the late ser Andreas Quirino, 4 May 1365.

302. Civeçel de Fosalta, son of the late ser Thobertus de Fosalta, *civis Tarvisanus, contestabilis equester pro comuni Venetiarum*, 6 August 1366.

303. Manfredinus, *soldatus comunis Venetiarum*, son of Bonasudhus de Stanchario, *de Feraria*, 6 December 1365.

304. Petrus Gulielmo, 30 January 1338.

305. Nicolaus Languvardo, *peliparius*, son of Georgius, 29 March 1341.

306. Marçoli, wife of Antonius Masaro, daughter of the late Marcus Muçio, 23 April 1341.

307. Clareta, daughter of the late Marcus Deso, wife of Ianulus Venerio, 11 May 1341.

308. Marudalena, widow of Marcus de Bonohomo, 15 March 1341.

309. Thomasina, daughter of the late Iacobus Caravela, 23 July 1341.

310. Iacobina, daughter of Georgius Languvardo, wife of Albertus de Savimonis, *ianuens*, 18 June 1342.

311. Bartholomeus de Hengelardis, 5 September 1342.

312. Nicolota de Venetiis, 6 October 1342.

313. Mariçoli, wife of Franciscus Marcii, 5 January 1342/43.

314. Gratiadeus Granela, 29 November 1343.

315. Plançaflore, widow of Iacobus Fuscolo, 5 January 1343/44.

316. Agnes, daughter of the late Iacobus Caravela, 9 February 1345/46.

317. *Magister* Gregorius de Spinis de Laudis, 7 January 1342/43.

318. Maria, widow of Adam de Vincentia, 6 July 1343.

319. Maria, widow of Riçardus Vasalo, 5 April 1346.

320. Çusamana, wife of Antonius Pascaligo, 15 January 1345/46.

321. Constantia, widow of Nicolaus Dono, 27 November 1346.

322. Margarita, wife of Georgius Çanpari, *faber*, 12 August 1347.

323. Palma, wife of Nicolaus Albiço, 11 January 1347/48.

324. *Presbyter* Petrus Dandulo, *capelanus ecclesie Crete*, 15 January 1347/48.

325. Antonia, widow of *dominus* Andreas Barocio, 19 April 1348.

326. Francisca, daughter of the late Stephanus Bono and wife of Matheus Gradonico, 28 March 1348.

327. Philippa, widow of Marcus Vidho, *murarius*, 31 December 1347.

328. Iacobus Paulo, *divisus* son of Marcus Paulo, 1 February 1347/48.

329. Angeloti, daughter of the late Iohannes Gisi, wife of Thomas Fradhello, 21 February 1346/47.

330. Franciscus, son of the late Bartholomeus Brixiano, *peliparius*, 10 May 1348.

331. Salera, daughter of the late Palencius de Verona, 17 March 1348.

332. Andreas Moro, son of the late Thomasinus Moro, 9 May 1347.

333. Nicolaus Catelan, *peliparius*, 1 June 1349.

334. Marinus Çanbon, *sellarius*, 10 September 1349.

335. *Presbyter* Lucas Mudacio, *canonicus Archadiensis*, 27 April 1349.

336. Potha, wife of Linchiachus Plumari, *iudeus*, 24 June 1319.

337. Marcus Baroci, 8 March 1319.

338. Maria de Molino, 23 September 1318.

339. Sibilia, wife of Marcus Columpna, 6 January 1318/19.

340. Iacobina, wife of Iohannes Clugia, daughter of the late Dominicus de Clugia, 28 Aug 1316.

341. Herini, daughter of Rebi Leo, *iudeus*, wife of Helias, son of the late Mardachay, 7 September 1320.

342. Iacobus Raguseus, 2 August 1320.

343. Maria, wife of *dominus* Marcus Faletro, 29 November 1326.

344. Agnes, wife of Iohannes Quirino, 20 May 1327.

345. Auroplase, widow of *dominus* Iacobus Baroci of Venice, 20 November 1329.

346. Amoratus Quirino, 3 June 1326.

347. Nicolaus Dompno, 9 February 1316/17.

348. Brutius de Sanctoro, *hab. Messani, insule Scicilie*, 9 March 1317.

349. Moyses, son of the late Leo Cali, *iudeus*, 23 May 1318.

350. Kerana, wife of Linchiachus, *iudeus*, 21 June 1317.

351. Daria, wife of Paulus Quirino, 25 May 1318.

352. Bartholomeus Venerio, *preco curie Crete*, 11 December 1325.

353. Angeliera, wife of Iohannes Rodolfo, 15 September 1312.

354. Maria, widow of Michael Barbo, 4 November 1312.

355. Soy, wife of Laurentius Caravella, 5 October 1325.

356. Stamatini, wife of Iohannes Iustiniano, 3 February 1325/26.

357. Heleni, wife of Iohannes de Carturio, 29 June 1327.

358. Nicolaus Cornario, son of Andreas Cornario Cornaroli, 15 September 1327.

359. Placentia, widow of Petrus Caravella, 21 March 1325.

360. Thomasina, wife of Gulielmus de Nigroponte, 5 January 1325/26.

361. Michali Serfioti, 6 December 1328.

362. Michaletus Simitecollo, *cerdo*, 6 October 1339.

363. Violenda Popo, widow of Iohannes Popo, 23 December 1341.

364. Leonardus Firiolo, March 1316.

365. Maria, wife of Frangullus Catalano, 3 May 1316.

366. Iacobina, wife of Marinus Longo, 4 June 1316.

367. Çenser, *baila* of *dominus* Paulus Donato, 22 April 1317.

368. Ysabeta, wife of Victor Alberto, 12 August 1317.

369. Aniça, wife of Petrus Trivixano, 8 August 1318.

370. Thomasina, widow of Michael Litigo, *hab. casalis Nogia*, 7 March 1320.

371. Agnes, widow of Thomas Fradelo, 26 July 1320.

372. Iacobina, wife of Marcus Raguseo, 11 November 1322.

373. Agnes, wife of Nicoletus Garabaro, 16 September 1322.

374. Mariçoli, wife of Nicoletus Çordanino, 24 October 1322.

375. Iohannes Quirino, *spatarius*, 24 April 1323.

376. Marinus Barbadico, 7 July 1323.

377. Agnes Brexiano, widow of Guiellmus Brexiano, *pilliparius*, date unknown, 1350.

378. Fantinus Superantio, *hab. Venetiarum in confinio Sancte Marie* [...], 26 September 1325.

379. Nicolaus Stamarino, *olim de confinio Sancti Severi de Venetiis*, 3 March 1326.

380. Maria, wife of Franciscus Caucina, 14 January 1319/20.

381. Thomasina Tonisto, sister of the Order of St Clara, 18 March 1316.

382. Fredericus de Ragusio, 24 November 1317.

383. Morisina de Portu, widow of Thomas de Portus, 16 February 1321/22.

384. Maria, wife of Antonius Belacura, daughter of Iohannes Mestrapiero, *cerdo*, 18 December 1331.

385. Leo Vradhiano, *hab. in casali Angela*, 17 January 1330/31.

386. Minoti Longo, widow of Nicolaus Longo, 15 October 1332.

387. Marchesina, wife of Nicolaus de Firmo, *notarius*, 5 February 1316/7.

388. Potha Calergi, widow of Leo Calergi, *hab. in casali Nasuvari*, 16 June 1343.

389. Phylippa Cornario, widow of Constantinus Cornario, 20 February 1347/48.

390. Angelus Belli, son of the late Marinus Belli, 6 October 1332.

391. Bonafacius de Boiardis of Ruberio, *comestabilis equester*, 7 May 1375.

392. Maria, wife of Nicolaus Tonano, *frenarius*, 24 May 1323.

393. Helena, widow of Antonius Psiruchi, 7 March 1322.

394. Agnes, widow of Iacobus Burgundione, 26 December 1323.

395. Sophia, wife of Dominicus de Clugia, called Andrioti, daughter of the late Theodorus Masochopo, *hab. casalis Archanes*, 1 April 1320.

396. Fillartus Polliti, 30 April 1323.

397. Iohannes Catellanos, *custos*, 7 February 1326.

398. Milliorina, widow of Marinus Vidho, 11 July 1322.

399. Iohannes Vergici, son of the late *papas* Petrus Vergici, 16 February 1322/23.

400. Caterina, daughter of Nicolaus de Plasença, *aurifex*, wife of Iohannes Rapani, 12 February 1323/24.

401. Cali, widow of Petrus Fovea, wife of Michael Dochanos, 4 July 1323.

402. Chiarana, widow of Iacobus Sclavo, 11 May 1329.

403. Andreas Tonello, 16 August 1333.

404. Iacomina, widow of Iohannes Longovardo, 5 August 1324.

405. Challi, wife of Philippus Orso, 19 November 1324.

406. Agnes, widow of Marinus Grasso, 24 March 1321.

407. Challi, widow of Arianus Contareno of Venice, 22 May 1325.

408. Thomasina, wife of Pasqualis Sclença, 24 September 1328.

409. Çanina, wife of Bertucius Matherelo of Venice, 23 November 1331.

410. Costa Petronicola, 18 February 1329/30.

411. Chali, former slave of Nicolaus Vasmulo, now free, 14 November 1329.

412. Mariçoli, widow of Bonifacius Trivisano, *sutor*, 22 March 1324.

413. Bonafemena, wife of Petrus Venerio, 5 March 1331.

414. Nicola, son of the late *papas* Hemanuel Agapito, 17 July 1331.

415. Marina, widow of Nicolaus Çancaruolo, 27 August 1331.

416. *Magister* Petrus da Rodhe, eldest son of the late Benvegnutus de Rodhe, 20 October 1331.

417. Agnes, daughter of the late *nobilis vir dominus* Alexius Calergi, wife of Chornarachus Cornario, 9 February 1330/31.

418. Stephanus Bono, *notarius*, 27 September 1331.
419. Sophia, wife of Bartholomeus Cavaler, daughter of the late *papas* Hemanuel Agapito, 3 November 1331.
420. Nicolaus Saxo, 13 January 1331/32.
421. Bonafanta, wife of Matheus Geno, 27 January 1331/32.
422. Herini, former slave of Petrus Lio, now free, wife of Stephanus Nigro, 2 April 1332.
423. Maria Romanitissa, wife of Ianullus de Nigroponte, 28 June 1332.
424. Herini Charadina, wife of Georgius Sichini *da ca' Çeno*, 25 February 1331/32.
425. Cecilia, widow of Antonius Habramo, 16 April 1337.
426. Mariçoli, wife of Marcus Barbadico, 7 May 1333.
427. Iohannes Balduino, 10 August 1337.
428. Nicolota Sovrançeo, daughter of the late Iohannes Superancio, 31 August 1337.
429. Petrus Greco, 17 September 1337.
430. Nichita Adhamo, 29 March 1337.
431. Nicolaus de Misina, *corteler*, 10 January 1337/38.
432. Richioldia, wife of Petrus Greco, 6 August 1335.
433. Maria Cuffopulina, widow of Costa, *seler*, of Constantinople, 5 July 1337.
434. Iohannes de Spoleto, 2 July 1338.
435. Maria, adopted daughter of Nicolaus Calderero, wife of Michael Calderero, former slaves of Nicolaus, 3 October 1338.
436. Michael Stadhiati called Mauro, 23 October 1338.
437. Agnes, daughter of the late Iohannes Trivisano, *murarius*, wife of Bartholomeus Onufri, *sutor*, 2 September 1338.
438. Nicolaus Avonale, *marangonus*, 2 August 1338.
439. Viola, widow of Franciscus Contareno of Venice, 14 April 1336.
440. Iohannes de Rugerio, natural son of Paulus de Rugerio, 8 September 1340.
441. Maria, widow of Marcus Caucho, 30 March 1339.
442. Magdalena, daughter of the late Marcus Caucho, 27 October 1339.
443. Nicolota, wife of Bartholomeus de Alexandro, *hab. in casali Sillamo*, 16 May 1340.
444. Marcus Francho, *barbitonsor*, 30 June 1340.
445. Helena, wife of Petrus Paulo, *faber*, daughter of the late Nicolaus Naptopuli of Caronissi, 11 May 1339.
446. Helena, daughter of the late Petrus Balastro, wife of Antonius Pispola, 19 May 1338.
447. Costa Vitalis, *incantator*, 11 May 1340.
448. Iohannes Bectaro, *hab. in episcopatu Hyro*, 21 October 1337.
449. Michale Cloni, 3 April 1330.
450. Xenus Doto, former slave of Matheus Doto, now free, 13 October 1330.
451. Balduinus Signolo, 14 November 1331.
452. Marcarius, *monacus*, *trogianus*, 25 March 1332.
453. Bartholomeus de Militibus, 9 April 1332.
454. Aniça, wife of Georgius Cornario, *arcerius*, 29 March 1332.
455. Agnes, wife of Victor Taiapetra, 21 September 1332.
456. Yonigha, widow of Petrus Dono, 15 February 1332/33.
457. Leo Metachieristi, 9 March 1333.
458. Dimitrius Thalasino, 5 September 1333.

459. *Papas* Iani Tricha, 12 October 1333.
460. Nicolota, wife of Çacharia Vendelino, 28 February 1333/34.
461. Maria, daughter of the late Thomas Avonale, *hab. in casali Colena*, 15 January 1333/34.
462. Thomasina, daughter of the late Thomas Avonale, *hab. in casali Colena*, 15 January 1333/34.
463. Anastassia, *iudea*, wife of Iecudha Balbi, *speciarius, iudeus*, 24 June 1334.
464. Maria, widow of Georgius Saclichi, called Caçomata, 3 January 1330/31.
465. Marchesina, wife of Marcus Sclavo, 24 December 1334.
466. Iohannes Ialina, son of the late *papas* Nichiforus Ialina, 31 March 1333.
467. Nicolaus Albi, son of the late Iohannes Albi, 16 January 1334/35.
468. Cali, wife of Iohannes Suriano called Capelus, 31 January 1335.
469. Iulianus Natale, 9 March 1334.
470. Herini, widow of Iohannes Mudaço, 30 or 31 [...] 1332.
471. Seti, *iudea*, wife of Moyses, son of the late Xenus, *iudeus*, 25 November 1332.
472. Aniça, wife of Hemanuel Chisamiti, 23 July 1339.
473. Thodorus Cafato, 11 August 1339.
474. Cheranna, *iudea*, widow of Curtesus, 24 February 1347/48.
475. Iohannes Brogondiono, 1 October 1343.
476. Phylippus Paulo, 27 December 1337.
477. *Papas* Iohannes Gesse, 2 February 1337/38.
478. Petrus Çangisti, *aurifex*, 19 January 1338/39.
479. Iohanninus Gisi, son of the late ser Marcus Gisi, 9 February 1338/39.
480. Stephanus Capelario, *hab. in castro Themensis*, 14 August 1339.
481. Barbara, wife of ser Donatus Trivixano of Venice, daughter of the *nobilis vir* Nicolaus de Polis of Venice, 30 May 1341.
482. Agnes, widow of ser Iohannes Vaxallo, son of the late ser Iulianus, daughter of the late ser Iohannes Caliva, 7 October 1341.
483. Lio Taliapetra, former slave of Matheus Taliapetra, now free, 13 June 1342.
484. Phylippus Bono, *butiglarius*, 13 May 1343.
485. Nicolaus Franco, son of the late Paulus Franco, 6 December 1343.
486. Bernardus Baboto, *catelanus*, 22 April 1343.
487. Nicolaus Beli, 31 March 1343.
488. Viola, widow of ser Petrus Venetando, 4 May 1343.
489. Anatalinus de Ranerio, 2 May 1343.
490. Iacobus Caravelo, 29 September 1342.
491. Aniça, daughter of the late Nicolaus Caluci, 4 June 1343.
492. Chimefti, *iudea*, widow of Rubin, *iudeus*, 17 June 1343.
493. Hergina Bocontolo, daughter of the late ser Philipus Bocontolo, wife of Bonifacius de Vigoncia, 24 June 1343.
494. Efdhoquia, daughter of the late Iohannes Cambaluri, 29 May 1343.
495. Francisca, wife of Belignus Dandulo, 25 June 1343.
496. Helena, daughter of the late *dominus* Donatus Dandulo, 2 September 1343.
497. Benedictus Iulianus, 19 November 1343.
498. Petrus Dono, son of the late dominus Paulus Dono, *hab. casalis Scalare*, 20 January 1346/47.

499. Herini, *iudea*, wife of Elia, *iudeus*, 14 March 1348.

500. Kali, widow of Theodorus Rapani, 11 July 1347.

501. Nicoletus Filaretis, 20 March 1348.

502. Heregina, *iudea*, wife of Moyses, *iudeus*, son of the late Salachagio, *iudeus*, 17 March 1348.

503. Bartholomeus Çorçano, *calafatus*, 14 March 1348.

504. Mathea, wife of Marinus Pantalio, *frenarius*, 17 March 1348.

505. Advenans de Molino, widow of ser Iohannes der Molino, 16 March 1348.

506. Katarina, wife of Petrus de Vicencia, 26 March 1348.

507. Maricioli, daughter of the late Nicoletus Geno, *barbitonsor*, 28 March 1348.

508. Gulialmus de Piamonte, *cerdo*, 19 March 1348.

509. Agnes, wife of Leonardus de Vegla, *notarius*, 19 March 1348.

510. Dominica, widow of Franciscus Pisani, 22 March 1348.

511. Salachagia, *iudeus*, son of the late Yeremia, *iudeus*, 6 April 1348.

512. Nicoletus Minoto, 19 January 1347/48.

513. Agnes, widow of Marcus Quirino, 27 March 1348.

514. Heregina, *iudea*, wife of Moyses, *iudeus*, son of the late Salachagia, *iudeus*, 17 March 1348.

515. Cali, widow of Theodorus Rapani, 11 July 1347.

516. Michael Chanioti, 24 March 1348.

517. Antonius Sclavo, son of the late Martinus, 20 March 1348.

518. Michael Paramandi, 1 April 1348/49.

519. Mariçoli, wife of Alexandrinus Spiron, 2 March 1348.

520. Katerina, wife of *dominus* Fantinus Pasqualigo of Venice, now *iudex Proprii Candide*, 1344 Jun 28.

521. Michaletus Bragadino *de confinio Sancti Ieminiani de Venetiis, nunc habitator Candide*, 18 March 1348.

522. Georgius, *magistri Victoris, physici*, 19 October 1342.

523. *Presbyter* Andreas Fuschi, *archidiaconus et canonicus Gerapetrensis*, 17 January 1342.

524. Frangulla, widow of Leonis Xidha, 22 March 1348.

525. Maria Grimani, widow of *dominus* Franciscus Grimani, 23 March 1348.

526. Mariçoli, widow of *magister* Gregorius, *ciruycus, de Spinis, de Laude*, 31 March 1348.

527. *Soror* Bertolota, *monacha monasterii Sancti Georgii*, 6 April 1344.

528. Georgius Selopullo, son of the late Moscoleus Selopullo, *hab. Ambrusie*, 31 March 1343.

529. Donatus Truno, 4 March 1348.

530. Vendramus Pilliça, 11 March 1348.

531. Iohannes Latura, 4 March 1348.

532. Agnes, widow of ser Thomas Paulo, 16 July 1367.

533. Thomasinus Sancti, 7 March 1366.

534. Agnes Mucio, 30 December 1366.

535. Nicolaus Venetando, son of the late ser Sergius, 3 September 1366.

536. Elena, widow of ser Marcus Dandulo, 26 July 1369.

537. Cheranna Casanena, 31 March 1375.

538. Nicolaus de Mello, 27 October 1375.

539. Alise Cauco, widow of ser Andreas Cauco, 9 October 1366.

540. Agnes Donçorçi, 16 June 1366.
541. Nicolaus Gligoropulo, *hab. in casali Ambrussia*, 21 December 1366.
542. Dominica Traversario, 26 January 1362/63.
543. Marinus Pasqualigo, son of the late ser Laurencius, 15 March 1376.
544. Iohannes Dandulo, son of the late *dominus* Marcus, 18 March 1376.
545. Michatius Damiano, *sutor*, 10 September 1373.
546. Marcus Mileo, *calogerus, hab. in casali Ambrussia*, 27 November 1368.
547. Marchesina, wife of ser Stamatus de Portu, 25 May 1365.
548. Marçoli, wife of ser Antonius Faletro, 17 October 1369.
549. Michali Pantalio, *hab. in casali Crussiona*, 7 October 1370.
550. Marchesina, wife of Georgius Aplada, 14 March 1370.
551. Georgius Prachimi, *fusarius*, 17 April 1366.
552. *Papas* Nicolaus Siropulo, 25 July 1376.
553. Hemanuel Suriano, *furnarius*, 27 July 1376.
554. Maria Quirino, wife of ser Nicolaus Quirino, 2 March 1376.
555. Maria Sanuto, 12 December 1376.
556. Angeloti Habramo, wife of Iacobus Habramo, 4 October 1375.
557. Petrus de Grimaldo, son of the late ser Iohannes, 7 October 1375.
558. Margarita Calergi, 2 July 1377.
559. Costas Davallerio, 30 May 1378.
560. Honesta Taliapetra, wife of ser Nicolaus Taliapetra, 23 December 1373.
561. Antonius de Piamonte, 17 March 1376.
562. Maria, wife of Michael, *famulus* of ser Christoforus de Bartholomeo, 14 March 1376.
563. Marula, wife of Iohannes Mussuro, *cerdo*, 11 February 1375.
564. Caterucia Baroci, wife of ser Andreas Baroci, 5 March 1374.
565. Iacoba, wife of Michael Urso of Candia, 4 July 1375.
566. Herchiolda Calergi, 8 October 1375.
567. Thomas Bollani, son of the late ser Thomas, 17 December 1375.
568. Franchus Visintino, 30 December 1373.
569. Iohannes Habramo, son of the late *dominus* Marinus Habramo, 18 December 1375.
570. Donatus Truno, son of the late ser Donatus, 14 February 1375/76.
571. Iohannes Longo of Venice, *admiratus*, 17 August 1383.
572. Hergina, widow of Achiles de Vicencia, 26 April 1348.
573. *Presbyter* Nicolaus Milovani, 17 April 1350.
574. Nicolaus de Milano, *notarius*, 5 November 1374.
575. Aniça Greco, wife of ser Dominicus Greco, 11 April 1375.
576. Cheranna, wife of Georgius Foca, 2 November 1375.
577. Sophia Grimaldena, 26 November 1375.
578. Katerina Gretola, widow of ser Iohannes Gretola, 21 November 1375.
579. Georgius Suriano, 26 December 1375.
580. Dondade Erizo, 12 January 1375/76.
581. Hemanuel Paulopulo, 10 June 1373.
582. Hellena, wife of Lappus de Florentia, *provisionatus in stipendio soldatorum equestrium Candide*, 22 February 1375/76.
583. Albertus de Verona, *stipendiarius equester Candide*, 26 February 1375/76.

584. Marcus de Bernardo, son of the late ser Paulus of Venice, 1 March 1376.

585. Iohannes Cornario, son of the late *dominus* Petrus of Venice, 2 March 1376.

586. Morellus de Forlivio, *comestabilis pedester Candide*, 3 March 1376.

587. Francus de Rugerio, 6 March 1376.

588. Anniza de Mulino, wife of ser Frangulius de Mulino, son of the late ser Hemanuel , 2 February 1375/76.

589. Georgius Pisani, son of the late *dominus* Nicolaus Pisani *de confinio Sancti Fantini de Venetiis*, 30 March 1376.

590. Iacobus Baroci, son of the late ser Marinus, 2 April 1376.

591. Petrus Cutaioti, son of the late ser Constantius, 1 May 1376.

592. Nicolaus Romeopulo, 15 June 1376.

593. Maria Sancti, 10 June 1377.

594. Matheus Tarono, *de confinio Sancti Petri de Castello de Venetiis*, 10 September 1377.

595. Anniça, wife of ser Nicolaus Cavalaro, 8 March 1378.

596. Marinus Gisi, son of the late ser Nicolaus and brother of the late ser Georgius, 17 February 1383.

597. Ursa, wife of ser Donatus de Molino, son of the late *dominus* Franciscus, 8 September 1386.

598. Cristina, daughter of the *egregius dominus* Lodovicus Mauroceno, *honorabilis Capitanei Crete*, widow of *dominus* Antonius Mauroceno, 15 August 1388.

599. Nicolaus Donçorçi called Cuculino, 18 September 1388.

600. Cali, widow of Nicolaus Vido, *barbitonsor*, 14 June 1362.

601. Erini, daughter of the late Georgius Pelecano, 22 June 1362.

602. Theodorus Alimussi, 26 May 1362.

603. Sifiossini, *calogrea*, widow of Nicolaus Sclavo, *murarius*, 23 May 1362.

604. Malgarita, widow of Costa Modhino, 14 June 1362.

605. Ergina, wife of Iohannes de Carturio, 26 May 1362.

606. Katerina, wife of Angelus Quirino, *christianus*, 18 May 1362.

607. Luludhia Chastarena, *calogrea*, 22 June 1362.

608. Dimitrius Pasqualigo de Nigroponte, 10 June 1362.

609. Katerina, daughter of the late Leo Anaplioti, 9 July 1362.

610. Mariçoli, daughter of the late ser Angelus Secreto, 6 June 1362.

611. Benedicta, wife of Iohannes de Vlero, 10 June 1362.

612. Ergina, daughter of ser Bartholomeus de Grimaldo, wife of ser Petrus Gradonico, 22 June 1362.

613. Iohannes Segredho, former slave of ser Iohannes Segredho, 15 October 1362.

614. Gligorus Anafioti, *mensurator*, 14 November 1362.

615. Donança, widow of Thomasinus Çafredo of Venice, 20 November 1362.

616. Antonius Vicentino, 10 April 1352.

617. Anastassu, wife of Michael Segredho, *preco*, 20 January 1362.

618. Cali Pronicadhena, 30 January 1362/63.

619. Petrus de Catania, *specialis*, 20 March 1363.

620. Ser Benedictus de Millano, 27 June 1362.

621. Maria, widow of Angelus Trignan, 15 May 1363.

622. Calli, wife of Iohannes Cornario, 23 May 1363.

623. Marcus Sclavo, son of the late Nicolaus, 25 June 1363.
624. Marula, wife of ser Iohannes de Gradu, 16 December 1359.
625. Georgius Selopulo, *aurifex*, 7 January 1359/60.
626. Laurencius de Soleis, *fornarius*, 17 June 1360.
627. Georgius Geno, son of the late Iohannes Geno, 19 October 1360.
628. Herini Iustiniano, *venderigola*, 14 July 1360.
629. Maria, widow of Iohannes Modhino, *monacha*, 15 May 1361.
630. Agnes, widow of ser Signoretus Betto, 21 May 1362.
631. Thomasina, daughter of Iacobus Donato, 23 May 1362.
632. Praxia, *monacha*, widow of Georgius Prassino, 22 May 1362.
633. Margarita, daughter of the late Demitrius Fuscolo of Chorono, wife of Ianulius Sanuto, 26 May 1362.
634. Soy, wife of Michaletus Rosso, *preco*, 19 March 1360.
635. Petrus Çane da Mantoa, *spatarius*, 5 June 1362.
636. Antonius Greco, 9 June 1362.
637. Aniça, widow of Petrus Çane da Mantoa, *spatarius*, 10 June 1362.
638. Herini, *iudea*, widow of Sambathus Chasuri, *iudeus*, 11 March 1348.
639. Fontana, widow of Antonius de Canali, 17 April 1348.
640. Katarina, wife of Marcus Venerio, son of the late ser Petrus Venerio, 16 March 1348.
641. Agnes, widow of Thomasinus Moro, 2 March 1348.
642. Marchesina, widow of Michael Beto, date unknown.
643. Hellea, *iudea*, wife of Ellia de Nigroponte, *iudeus*, 27 January 1351.
644. Hemanuel Venetando, son of the late ser Sergius Venetando, 7 March 1351.
645. Nida, widow of *dominus* Petrus Venerio, 6 March 1348.
646. Iohannes Quirino, 25 June 1355.
647. Maria, widow of *magister* Vivianus, *cerdo*, 10 July 1355.
648. Archondisa, *iudea*, widow of Helias, *catellanus*, *iudeus*, 3 December 1358.
649. Hemanuel Cursari, 12 December 1358.
650. Bertucius Gradonico, son of the late ser Petrus Gradonico, 16 June 1362.
651. Agnes, widow of Nicolaus Chandachiti, *hab. in casali Caiafa*, 25 June 1362.
652. Margarita, widow of ser Iacobus de Vigoncia, 11 April 1348.
653. Iacobina, widow of Petrus Sclavo, 6 June 1351.
654. Barbara Nani, widow of *dominus* Iacobus Nani of Venice, *hab. Veneciis*, 3 March 1400.
655. Petrus Çimiacho, *de districtu Castri Mirabelli de casali vocato Psatha*, 10 January 1402/3.
656. Chalinichi Misinena, *chalogrea*, wife of ser Çanachius de Mesina, *hab. monasterii Sanctorum Apostolorum de Pigadulia*, 270 1408.
657. Richiolda, widow of *dominus* Andreas *de domo maiori*, 17 May 1408.
658. Palma, wife of the *nobilis vir* ser Michaletus Cornario, son of the late *dominus* Iohannes *de domo maiori*, 30 November 1412.
659. Maria, widow of *dominus* Iohannes Cornario, son of the late *dominus* Andreas *de domo maiori*, 11 November 1415.
660. Chaterucia Quirino, widow of ser Frangius Quirino, 28 January 1418/19.
661. Erini, wife of Hemanuel Candaquiti, *cilerarius*, 19 May 1398.
662. Marchesina Descamato, wife of Matheus Turco, 12 August 1406.

663. Helena, wife of Georgius Melaldo, *peliparius, hab. in casali Chaçaba*, 18 September 1407.
664. Dona Zoana Pasqualigo, wife of the *nobilis vir* Marinus Pasqualigo of Venice, 9 August 1409.
665. Marreta, wife of the *nobilis vir* ser Franciscus Bolan of Venice, 13 January 1409/10.
666. Agnes Bicontolo, widow of ser Philipus Bicontolo, 1 February 1409/10.
667. Iacobelus Lambardo, *marangonus*, 3 March 1412.
668. Andreas, son of the late *dominus* Petrus Duodo of Venice, 27 March 1412.
669. Nicolinus Maçamano, 21 February 1408/9.
670. Hergina, widow of Georgius Sclavo, 1 December 1343.
671. Dimitrius Draganno, 6 December 1413.
672. Marinela, wife of Paulus Faletro, 5 August 1414.
673. Marula, wife of ser Dominicus Castrofilacha, 3 October 1415.
674. Nicolaus Dadho, 19 July 1414.
675. Andreas Geno called Maurogonato, 2 January 1416/17.
676. Agnes, widow of *dominus* Zanachius Istrigo, 12 February 1416/17.
677. Iacoba, wife of ser Zaninus Dadho, 11 February 1416/17.
678. *Presbyter* Georgius Caucho, *venetus, cantor ecclesie Crete*, 2 July 1418.
679. Marinus Nuto, 20 February 1419/20.
680. Bonzuora, wife of ser Nasimbene de Çambono, daughter of the late ser Theodorus de Caliça, 11 September 1375.
681. Iacobina Bocontolo, widow of ser Angelus Bocontolo, 31 January 1375.
682. Aniça Lambardena, 20 February 1375/76.
683. Constancius Avonale, 16 March 1376.
684. Chali, wife of Leo Calogeropulo, 29 March 1376.
685. Margarita, wife of Cristoforus de Borgno, 28 March 1376.
686. Iohannes Garguli, son of the late ser Andreas, 3 April 1376.
687. Michaletus Maufredo, 4 April 1376.
688. Nicolaus da Madio of Venice, 18 March 1376.
689. Iacobellus Avonale, son of the late ser Constancius, 16 April 1376.
690. Sophia Papadia, wife of *papas* Constantinus tu Siriano, 23 April 1373.
691. Marcus Vasallo, son of the late ser Iohannes, 2 May 1376.
692. Iohannes Liverio, 23 May 1376.
693. Aniça Ruçino, wife of ser Marcus Ruçino of Venice, 29 July 1376.
694. Thomas Raguseo, son of the late ser Matheus, 22 August 1376.
695. Çaninus Manolesso, 14 September 1376.
696. Stamatius de Portu, son of the late ser Iohannes de Portu, 23 January 1376/77.
697. Mariçoli, widow of ser Paulus de Plubino, 13 December 1376.
698. Maria, wife of Iohannes Mauro, *aurifex*, 15 May 1377.
699. Iohannes Habramo, 16 May 1377.
700. Andriola de Cartore, widow of ser Nicolaus de Cartore, 29 December 1377.
701. Iohannes Fuscarino, son of the late ser Nicolaus, 8 December 1377.
702. Honesta, wife of Nicolaus Carandino, 20 June 1377.
703. Herigina, daughter of the late ser Nicolaus Venerio, wife of Simeon Greco, 20 March 1379.

704. Alexius Sarmea, *murarius*, 17 April 1379.
705. Parnatissa tu Carteru, *iudea*, 11 March 1379.
706. Andreas Torello, 1 May 1376.
707. Dimitrius Massaro, 27 January 1379/80.
708. Chali Savonario, widow of Iohannes Savonario, 5 February 1379/80.
709. *Nobilis vir* ser Bernardus Vituri of Venice, 27 April 1381.
710. Georgius Gritola, *preco,* 20 October 1381.
711. Mariçoli, wife of ser Andreas Bolani, 5 November 1381.
712. Georgius Stadioti, *hab. casalis Males*, 19 April 1381.
713. Marchesina, widow of ser Marinus Magno, 22 December 1381.
714. Fantina, wife of Hemanuel Thobono, *piscator*, 13 December 1381.
715. Bartholomeus Donno of Sithea, 8 April 1382.
716. Herigina, wife of ser Marinus Geno, 21 February 1381/82.
717. Lodovicus de Medio, son of the late *dominus* Iacobus de Medio of Venice, 23 June 1382.
718. Bernardus of Parma, 9 July 1382.
719. Helena, wife of Georgius Pascaligo, *cerdo*, 22 August 1382.
720. Georgius Mosco, *piliparius*, 7 September 1382.
721. Maria Cornario, widow of *dominus* Andreas Cornario, 10 October 1382.
722. Marcus Caucanigo, 24 October 1382.
723. Iohannes Pandecho, from the island of Gena, 5 October 1383.
724. Iohannes Spano, 21 September 1384.
725. Marinus Trivisano, son of the late *dominus* Victor Trivisano of Venice, 29 August 1380.
726. Caterina, widow of ser Marinus Quirino, 8 August 1365.
727. Aniça, wife of Petrus de Medio, 12 May 1365.
728. Dimitrius Caco, *hab. casalis Caiafa*, 9 May 1366.
729. Frosenda, widow of Marcus Gradonico, 31 May 1366.
730. Marchesina, widow of Andreas Pantalleo, 10 July 1366.
731. Georgius Langadioti, 14 September 1366.
732. Aniça Langovardena, 17 June 1364.
733. Marchesina Tanto, widow of ser Marcus Tanto, 12 May 1366.
734. Iohannes de Firmo, *notarius*, 22 December 1366.
735. *Papas* Nicolaus Castamoniti of Rethimno, *calogerus*, 1 June 1368.
736. Hemanuel Bono, son of the late ser Bartholomeus Bono, 16 February 1366/67.
737. Marula, wife of Matheus Mudacio, 25 November 1366.
738. Agnes, wife of ser Marcus Boldu, 24 May 1367.
739. Mariçoli, wife of ser Çanachius Ystrego, 25 April 1367.
740. Stamatina, daughter of Franghia Balastro, 7 February 1363/64.
741. Andreas de Vigoncia, son of the late ser Petrus, 2 May 1367.
742. Çaneta, wife of Iohannes de Çordano of Venice *coraçanus*, 11 March 1378.
743. Ysacharus, theotonicus, *iudeus*, 4 May 1378.
744. Martinus de Soldan, *marangonus*, of Venice, 29 August 1378.
745. Philippa, wife of ser Franciscus Foscareno, 18 December 1385.
746. Thomasina, widow of ser Michael de Ragusia, 2 April 1387.
747. Dimitrius Alexiopulo, 1385.
748. Michael Gradonico Besucho, 5 August 1385.

749. Anica, wife of Franculus Cauco Clida, 10 May 1383.

750. Ligiacus Casani, 30 June 1383.

751. Conço de Felchelcha, [..] September 1383.

752. Heleni Alexandrina, 20 November 1383.

753. Marula Chafatena, *hab. monasterii Sanctorum Apostolorum*, 11 August 1383.

754. Concionis Padurachi, 6 June 1385.

755. Cherana Armachena, 11 June 1385.

756. *Calogrea* Miradhia, *hab. monasterii Sancti Nicolai*, 20 February 1385/86.

757. Helena, wife of Gracias Granela, 23 March 1384.

758. *Calogrea* Paramadena, 29 March 1387.

759. Pasqualis Coroneo, 10 January 1386/87.

760. Laurentius Framarino, *preco*, 8 October 1384.

761. Michali Quirino, 14 March 1387.

762. Cherana, *iudea*, wife of David da la Chania, 25 December 1373.

763. Nicolaus Vurgari, 23 February 1373/74.

764. *Papas* Iohannes Callopulo, 31 March 1374.

765. Iohannes Mudacio Bicho, 5 March 1376.

766. Mariçoli, wife of ser Iohannes Iallina, 18 March 1376.

767. Gratonus Dandulo, *civis Venetiarum*, son of *dominus* Iohannes Dandulo, *miles*, 31 March 1376.

768. Phylippa, daughter of ser Dominicus Grimani, *cancellarius Crete*, wife of ser Georgius de Molino, 7 April 1376.

769. Phylippus Cornario, son of ser Marcus Cornario, 12 April 1376.

770. Magdalena, widow of ser Nicolaus Bono, 14 April 1376.

771. Andreas Maçamurdi, 4 April 1376.

772. Nicolaus Cornario, son of the late ser Iohannes, 20 May 1376.

773. *Papas* Nicolaus Metupa, 26 April 1376.

774. Nicolaus Dandulo, son of the late *dominus* Marcus Dandulo, 5 July 1376.

775. Magdalucia, widow of ser Michael Barbadico, 12 March 1376.

776. Matheus Gici, *hab. castri Sithye*, 28 August 1378.

777. Benedicta, widow of ser Sclavus Magno, 23 November 1377.

778. Mariçoli, widow of *dominus* Bampaninus Quirino, 15 September 1380.

779. Iohannes Baroci, son of the late *dominus* Marinus, 21 July 1380.

780. Ergina, wife of Georgius Sinadino, 23 September 1380.

781. Andreas deli Cavalieri, 21 October 1380.

782. Maria Papadia, widow of *papas* Nicolaus Metupa, 8 November 1382.

783. Elena, wife of ser Franciscus Dandulo, 20 June 1383.

784. Marcus Pispola, 23 April 1384.

785. Sabatheus Casani, *iudeus*, 26 April 1384.

786. Margarita, widow of Antonius de Trento, 20 September 1384.

787. Iohannes de Ania, 13 November 1384.

788. Calli Manolicena, 4 April 1381.

789. Marina, wife of *dominus* Nicolaus Çane, 28 November 1382.

790. Iacobus Pasqualigo of Venice, *hab. Rethimni*, 9 August 1392.

Index

Abbate, Abbatis
    Franciscus de, 705
    Gabriel de, 189
    Gabriel de, frater,
        provinciale Fratrum
        Heremitarum, 990
    Georgius de, 219, 279,
        383, 803, 920
    Iohannes de, 189
    Iohannes, son of Georgius
        de, 384
    Michael de, 803
    Marinus de, 705, 909
    Potha, widow of Iohannes,
        189
abbatessa, abbatissa
    Cornario, Marchesina, of
        S. Laurencius, 266
    Gradonico, Agnes, soror,
        939
Abbatia
    Leo de, 8
Abolis, 494
Abramo
    Agnes, 35, 110, 162, 863,
        799, 885
    Alvise, 55
    Angeloti, wife of Iacobus,
        702
    Aniça, 720
    Antonius, 109, 183, 196,
        551, 885
    Bartholomeus, 392
    Cali, wife of Hemanuel,
        aurifex, 16
    Cecilia, widow of
        Antonius, 551
    Donatus, 759
    Flori, natural daughter of
        Petrus, 183
    Frangula, wife of
        Nicolaus, 302
    Georgius, 689
    Gratia, daughter of
        Iohannes, 720
    Helena, 23
    Helena, widow of
        Nicolaus, 109

Hemanuel, 79, 302
Hemanuel, aurifex, 16
Herigina, daughter of
    Antonius, 885
Iacobina, wife of
    Nicolaus, 161
Iacobus, 23, 35, 702
Iohannes, 36, 55, 302,
    719, 786, 885
Leonardus, 22, 36, 382,
    480
Lianora, 382
Lodovicus, 720
Logdoycus, 302
Marchesina, widow of
    Nicolaus, 182
Marçoli, 110
Marcus, 23, 110, 480,
    863
Mariçoli, daughter of
    Marcus, 23
Mariçoli, natural daughter
    of Nicolaus, 302
Marinus, 301, 719
Marinus, natural son of
    Petrus, 182
Mathio, 866
N., 833
Natale, 23, 36, 183
Nicolaus, 62, 109, 161,
    182, 183, 196, 301,
    551, 886
Nicoletus, 799
Pauletus, 183
Petrus, 36, 182, 252, 676
Philipa, 392
Philipa, daughter of
    Iacobus, 23
Philipa, daughter of
    Leonardus, 22
Philipa, soror, monacha,
    635
Potha, 885
Raphael, 62, 183, 196,
    302, 350, 799
venderigolus, 392
viduleta, 392
Vitalis, 392

Abramus
    frater, 93
Abrussia, see Ambrussia
Acardo
    Bartholomeus, 707
    Costa, 792
    Iohannes, 235, 272, 442
    Nicolaus, presbyter, 215,
        441
Achamia, 121
Achelena
    Belli, wife of Antonius,
        notarius, 535
Acheli
    Stamatinus, 647
Achieli, Achyli
    Leo, 577, 665
    Stamatini, wife of Leo,
        665
Achiles
    Vicencia, de, 724
Achulo
    Georgius, slave, 224
    Helena, wife of
        Theodorus de, 242
    Theodorus de, 242
Acladha
    Theodori, 804
Aço
    Iohannes, 478
Acon
    Bertulinus de, 265
    Nicolaus de, 265, 666
Açonibus
    Riçolinus de, of Tarvisio,
        contestabile equester,
        398
Acotanto
    Iohannes, of Sithia, 990
Acre
    Leonardus de, 212
    Mariçoli, wife of
        Leonardus, 212
Acriti, 578
Açupaduli
    monasterium, 284
Adam
    Vincentia, de, 421

Piseadena, 978
Portu, de ca', 302
Prachimi, wife of
Georgius, fusarius,
696
Praghamena, 948
Quirino, 869
Quirino, daughter of
Marinus, 84
Quirino, widow of
Marcus, 652
Quirino, wife of Georgius,
758
Quirino, wife of Iohannes,
453
Renaldena, 20
Renauldi, 568
Sclavo, 194, 229
Sclavo, daughter of
Çachetus, 631
Sclença, 269, 666
Segnolo, 224
Senedulo, soror, 210
Siropulo, 697
soror, monialis, 666
Staurachi, 427
Striviachiena, 814
tabernaria, 738
Taiapetra, wife of Victor,
586
Thalasino, daughter of
Iohannes, 604
Triandafilo, widow of
Iohannes, papas, 253
Vasilii, 746
Vasallo, daughter of
Marcus, 875
Vaxallo, widow of
Iohannes, 619
Vegla, wife of Leonardus,
notarius, 648
Venerio, 49
Venerio, daughter of
Angelus, 93
Venerio, daughter of
Dominicus, 93
Venerio, daughter of
Iohannes, 110

Venerio, daughter of
Nicolaus, 119, 225
Venerio, widow of
Nicolaus, 463
Vergici, 706
Vigoncia, natural
daughter of Petrus de,
919
visastra, 395
Zorzi, 342
Agnesina
Çulian, wife of Antonius
de, 989
Mauroceno, wife of
Lodovicus, 762
Agorerium, 640, 654
Agustinus
Gradonico, 318
Aitania
serventaria, 312
Aius Pandes
ecclesia, 846, 849
monasterium, 850
Alamano
Nicolaus, 553
Alani, 425
Alana
Maria, 327, 547
Maria, ex-slave, 487
Maria, slave, 579
Alba, 176, 287
Baxilio, wife of Raphael,
184
Belli, wife of Antonius,
99
Albani
Venetando, daughter of
Iohannes, 105
Albanis
Michael de, 102
Albanus
Baduario, ducha Crete,
831
Balduvino, 41, 161, 555
Albaxanus
Conte, magister, 770
Alberico
Georgius de, 8

Thomas de, 8
Albertinus, 472
Braçole, 652
Cornario, 204, 308
Geno, 907, 910
Maça, notarius, 412
Palamonte, 140
Riparius, father of
Benedictus,
clericus, 6
Alberto
Marchesina, wife of
Nicolaus, preco, 143
Nicolaus, preco, 143
Nicolota, 27
Victor, 484
Ysabeta, wife of Victor,
484
Albertus
Ferraria, de, 399
Maça, notarius, 76
Palamonte, 417, 602
Palamonte, notarius, 435
Porta, da la, 954
Savimonis, de, ianuens,
410
Verona, de, stipendiarius
equester, 738
Albi
Anna, 600
Antonia, 90
Boneta, daughter of
Nicolaus, 600
Hemanuel, 695, 696
Iohannes, 600
Iohannes, son of
Nicolaus, 600
Iulianus, son of Nicolaus,
600
Maricioli, daughter of
Nicolaus, 600
Marçoli, 90
Nicolaus, 600
Thomas, 225
Thomas, son of Nicolaus,
600
Vinturossa, 600
Albiano

Nicolinus de, 130

Albicinus
Casarolo, 393

Albiço
Andreas, 110
Antonius, presbyter, 66, 646
Antonius, diaconus, 421
Hemanuel, 427
Nicolaus, 427
Palma, wife of Nicolaus, 427

Alcana
Politi, iudeus, 215

Alchannus
Vilanovis, de, 24

Alcarmus
slave, 318

Aldigerus
Mantua, de, 392

Alefandini, 958
Geno, wife of Franciscus, 983

Alegratia
Mutio, widow of Marcus, 405

Alemana, 661
Fradello, wife of Marcus, 153

Alemanis
Franciscus de, magister, cirurgicus, 359

Alesandrino
Petrus, 599

Alevrandinus
Betto, 705

Alexadio
Agnes, 950

Alexander
Cortesella, de, 762
Bono of Venice, 897
Sancti, son of Marcus, 544
Senda, de, 58
Vassalo, 20
Vaxalo, 620

Alexandra
Helena, daughter of

Sperandeus de, 26, 598
Sperandeus de, 26, 598

Alexandrena
Helena, 705

Alexandria, 201, 300, 905
Bartholomeus de, 16
Chavi de, iudeus, 174
Chavi de, iudeus, 174
Eudochia de, iudea, 174
Iohannes de, 268, 515
Laurencius de, 843
Petrus de, 857

Alexandrina
Heleni, 945

Alexandrino
N., 625

Alexandrinus, 755
Franciscus, 8
Spiron, 659

Alexandrio
Nicolaus de, 19

Alexandro
Aniça, 856
Bartholomeus de, 27, 572
Beatrix, wife of
Dominicus de, 536
Cecilia de, 186
Dimitrius, 782
Dominicus de, 536
Elena, wife of Iohannes, 776
Helena de, 573
Iohannes, 13, 19, 98, 193, 448, 559, 776, 780, 782
Marcus de, 193
Nicolaus de, 263
Nicolota, wife of
Bartholomeus de, 572
Rubina de, 260
Stelleta, wife of Iohannes de, 448

Alexena
Cali, 169

Alexi
Chisamodi, son of
Stratigi, 953

Alexiopulo
Barbara, daughter of
Dimitrius, 940
Dimitrius, 940

Alexius, 946
Androcio, 54
Apochafcho, pretor, 839
Calergi, 172, 270, 541, 614
Carandino, 48
Cipro, de, 619
Cornario de domu maiori, 206, 226, 314, 331, 360
Corner, 330
Dandulo, son of
Nicolaus, 972
Gisi, 802, 915
Langovardo, 659
S., 151
Sarmea, murarius, 891
Suli, 162
Vigoncia, de, 919

Aligaça
Georgius, 73

Alimanus
Iohannes, 310
Maria, wife of Iohannes, 310

Alimussi
Constancia, daughter of
Theodorus, 768
Hemanuel, son of
Theodorus, 768
Maria, daughter of
Theodorus, 768
Potha, wife of Theodorus, 768
Sophia, daughter of
Theodorus, 768
Theodorus, 768
Thomaxina, daughter of
Theodorus, 768

Alisa, Alise, Alysa, 35, 103, 402, 418, 801
Belli, daughter of
Nicoletus, 488
Cauco, 682

Belli, daughter of Nicoletus, 488
  Cauco, 682
  Milovani, 233
Alissafi
  calogrea, 341
Alisse
  Turre, wife of Marcus de la, 384
Allcharinus
  Vilanova, de, 817
Alnevo
  Fosina, 679
Altadena
  wife of Leo, sutor, 37
Altariolum, 664
Altinerius
  Fosalta, de, 398
Altoflora, 531
Alvirandinus
  Beto, 154
Alvirando
  Andreas, 177, 287, 786
  Bartholomeus, 51, 77, 177, 205, 286
  Helena, widow of Matheus, 176
  Marcus, 150, 176
  Martinus, 4
  Matheus, 176
  Nicolaus, 150, 176
Alvirandus
  Bruno, 774
Alvise
  Abramo, 55
Amari
  serventaria, 539
Amarando
  Dimitrius, 854
  Eudochia, 710
Ambelioti
  Iohannes, 622
Ambani, 39
Ambava, 730
Ambelotopum, 222
Ambronorum
  casale, 118
Ambrusia

Casale, 135, 145, 240, 447, 670, 685, 691, 899
Amorgos, Murgo
  insula, 436
Anifandi
  Xeni, 534
Amico
  Nicolaus de, 604
  Nicoletus de, 596
  Petrus de, 304
  Zanachius de, 733
Amoratus, Amoretus
  Bocontolo, 41
  Quirino, 455, 977
Amoreta, 665
Amurgino
  Euginu, 769
  Marcus, 386
  Nicolaus, papas, 386
  Piffanius, son of Xeni, 769
  Xeni, 769
Amurgo, 615
  I. de, 28
Ana, see Anna
Anafio
  Hemanuel de, 680
Anafioti
  Cali, wife of Gregorius, 181
  Erina, wife of Gligorus, mensurator, 780
  Gligorius, mensurator, 780
  Gregorius, 181
Anafiotisa
  Maria, 188
  Sophia, 680
Anapli, 49
Anaplioti
  Caterina, daughter of Leo, 774
  Leo, 774, 797
  Maria, wife of Leo, 797
Anapliotissa
  Maria, called Çeni, 775
Anapoli, 946

Anastasia, Anastassa, 466
  Aucepis, wife of Donatus, 163
  Balbi, iudea, wife of Iecudha, iudeus, speciarius, 595
  slave, 725
Anastassa, see Anastasia
Anastassu, 491, 542, 633, 776
  Caravelo, widow of Nicolaus, 18
  Castamoniti, daughter of Iohannes, 926
  iudea, 300, 892
  Segredo, wife of Michael, preco, 783
  slave, 793
Anata
  Herini, 162
Anatalinus
  Ranerio, de, 627
Anbelachiano
  Nicolaus, 388
ancila
  Benevenuta, 212
  Blancia, 265
  Cali, 250
  Cherana, 191, 309
  Chrussia, 205
  Cureni, Aniça
  Moscana, 143
  Nicolota, 287
  Herini, 806
  Oltoni, 627
  Pliti, 262
  Theophanu, 154
  Turcopula, 230
ancilus
  Churssi, 309
Ançoleto
  nena, 553
Ançolo
  Michiel, 334
Ancona, 109, 314, 773
  Agnes, widow of Nutus de, 438
  Caterina de, 242

Geno, wife of Georgius, 795

Nutus de, 438

S. Iohannes Baptisa, 736

Andentiis

Michael de, spatarius, 611

Andianopolita

Iohannes, papas, 793

Andradhino

Michael, 622

Andreas, 251, 273, 388, 471, 486, 578, 607, 915, 980

Agapito, 38, 282

Albiço, 110

Alvirando, 177, 287, 786

Avonale, 595

Bafo de Rethimo, 273

Balduvino, son of Iohannes, 555

Barbadico, 643, 653

Barbarigo, 412

Barbo, 75

Barchis, de le, 633

Baroci, 313, 430, 683, 713, 749, 979

Barozi, admiratus imperii Romanie, 453, 454

Bellamore, de, 466

Bocanigo, peliparius, 404

Bocanigra, 419

Bollani, 103, 898,939

Bono, 71

Bononia, de, frater, prior, 393

Borocio, 154

Brexiano, 51

Brexiano, notarius, 49, 279

Calergi, 159, 271, 428

Calica, 717

Çambela, 688, 767, 768, 771, 773, 775, 779, 782, 784-786, 789

Capadhoca, 10

Capadoca, papas, 891

Caravello, natural son of Franciscus, 369

Catelano, 287, 330

Cauco, 180, 274, 441, 682, 742, 858, 859

Cauco, notarius, 850

Cavalero, 891

Cavalieri, de li, 981

Çeno, 572

Cesena, de, frater, lector Fratrum Minorum, 366, 371

Clarencia, de, 374

Conradine, 506

Contareno, 345

Contareno, called Zafuri, 850

Corario, 81, 106

Corer, 931

Corinthi, 738

Cornario, 26, 57, 62, 225, 250, 257, 262, 266, 271, 287, 331, 360, 364, 746, 861, 871, 898, 909, 956, 967, 993

Cornario Cornaroli, 471

Cornario de domu maiori, 833, 912

Cornario of Venice, 265

Cornario, son of Marcus, de domu maiori, 314

Curtalo, papas, 149

Dandulo, 259, 415, 504, 959, 972

Doto, frater, 454

Duodo, son of Petrus of Venice, 847

Duracio, de, 859

Feragudho, 601

Firgavesto, 609

Firmo, de, cancellarius Crete, 53, 60, 68, 69, 198, 272, 610, 644, 651-653, 655-660, 662

Flegotomo, 792

Fradello, 294

Fraganes, presbyter, 214

Fraganesco, 796

Fuschi, archidiaconus,

presbyter, canonicus gerapetrensis, 663

Fusculo, presbyter, 469

Gabriel, 222

Garguli, 869

Gasparino, 859

Geno, called Maurogonato, 854

Geno, ducha Crete, 975

Gisi, 145, 171, 172, 352, 821

Goro, 641, 655

Gradonico, 242, 259, 415, 577

Grimaldo, de, 703

Grimani, presbyter, 125

Iordano, de, 369, 412

Istrigo, 856

Iustiniano, 376

Iustiniano de Venetiis, 71, 385

Luroto, villanus, 706

Maçamurdi, 965

Manolesso, 378

Maripetro, 275

Matono, 541, 845

Mauro, 592

Michael, 696

Moro, 439

Moroni, 693

Morono, 222

Mucio, 230

Nani, son of Belellus, 359

Otobono, 503

Pantaleo, 68, 69, 223, 234, 259, 271, 539, 577, 705, 921

Pantaleo, son of Iacobus, 539

Pantaleo, widow of Andreas, 259

Pantaleo maior, 17

Pantaleo, presbyter, 256, 259

Pantalio, 415, 440, 941

Pantalio Pichimili, 857, 858

Papadhopulo, 622

Venetando, 104

Angelinus
  frater, episcopus Sude,
    273
Angelo
  Antonius de, 160
Angelota
  soror, 210
Angeloti
  Fradello, wife of Thomas,
    435
Angelus, 422, 529, 699
  Baduario de Venetiis, 398
  Barbadico, 968, 974
  Belli, 509
  Beraldo, 243, 802
  Biaqua, 675, 678
  Bocontolo, 863
  Borgognono, 964, 969
  Brogogno, 252
  Brogognono, son of
    Marcus, 342
  Brugondione, 539
  Caravella, 196, 259, 473
  Caravello, 84, 630
  Contareno, 557
  Deso, diaconus, 406
  Gisi, 186
  Leocari, 258
  Marçangelo, 691
  Marçangelo, son of
    Nicolaus, 219
  Mucio, 592
  Neapoli, de, 785
  Pascaligo, 869
  Paulopulo, 735
  pilicer, 579
  Quirino, 235, 280, 307,
    351, 397, 672, 774,
    778, 787, 892, 894
  Quirino, christianus, 771
  Salamon, 583
  Secreto, 680, 775
  Tadaudo, 56
  Tedaldo, 481
  Tedaldo, peliparius, 403
  Traversario, 869
  Trignan, 787

Vano, de, 217
Venerio, 93
Venetando, frater, 93,
    627
Vigoncia, de, 209, 291,
    920, 934
Anglese
  Basilius, 503
Angelidhi
  Michael, papas, 467
  Moscana, widow of
    Michael, papas, 467
Anguro
  Samargias, 579
Ania
  Filipus de, 434
  Helena, daughter of
    Iohannes de, 991
  Helena, wife of Filipus
    de, 434
  Iohannes de, 990
  Maria, daughter of
    Iohannes de, 991
  Marula, wife of Iohannes
    de, 990
Aniça, Anicia, Anniça, 10, 16,
    90, 95, 257, 269, 294,
    306, 328, 428, 461, 481,
    513, 549, 574, 640, 654,
    730, 758, 772, 788, 802,
    804, 992
  Alexandro, 856
  Avonale, 390
  baiula, 57, 366, 909
  Balastro, 157, 408, 434
  Balduvino, natural
    daughter of Albani,
    41
  Bocontolo, 30
  Calergi, daughter of
    Marcus, marescalcus,
    207
  Caluci, daughter of
    Nicolaus, 630
  Çane, widow of Petrus,
    da Mantua, spatarius,
    805, 807
  Carandino, wife of

Michael, 237
Caselato, widow of
    Bigotius, 440
Cassellarena, 701
Catalieno, 552
Caucanigo, wife of
    Marcus, 910
Cauco Clida, 943
Cavalaro, wife of
    Nicolaus, 757
Cavalcante, natural
    daughter of
    Dominicus, 273
Cheretena, 852
Chiloplenna, 622
Chisamiti, wife of
    Hemanuel, 606
Choronea, 939
Cirita, wife of Antonius,
    caligarius, 50
Copella, 508
Cornario, 833, 835
Cornario, wife of
    Georgius, arcerius,
    585
Crasudhi, daughter of
    Vasili, 77
Cristina, monaca, nena,
    54
Cureni, ancila, 233
Cursari, wife of
    Hemanuel, 822
Diminitis, daughter of
    Georgius, 802
famula, 11
Fontanela, 18
Garguli, 869
Geno, 854
Gradonico, 158
Habramo, 720
Ialina, wife of Iohannes,
    228, 231
Lambardena, 864
Langovardena, 922
Lathura, sister of
    Hemanuel, 52
Marçangelo, wife of
    Nicolaus, 218

Aquilo
  Marcus de, 43
  Marinus de, 43
Ara
  Antonius, son of Marcus,
    870
  Hemanuel, 245, 438, 555
  Iohannes, 903
  Marcus, 801, 870
Aradhena
  Eudhochia, 79
aranda, 347
Arasmolus
  Mediolano, de, soldatus,
    400
Aravona, 527
Arbe
  Georgius de, 976
Arcadhi
  casale, 225
arcella, 29, 78, 183, 414, 526,
  684, 785
arcerius
  Chandachyti, Michael,
    305
  Cornario, Georgius, 585
  Fodhelo, Nicolaus, 4
  Iohannes, 74
  Marcus, 306
archa, 473
Archadiensis, Archadyensis
  ecclesia, 859
  episcopus, 568
  Mudacio, Lucas,
    presbyter, canonicus,
    442
Archanes, Archanis
  casale, 516
  serventaria, 671
Archari
  contrata, 727
Archens
  logo, 962
Archidiaconus
  Fuschi, Andreas,
    presbyter,
    gerapetrensis, 663
archiepiscopus Crete, 25, 103,

158, 567
Archioldus, 635
Archistratigi
  ecclesia, 757
Archondissa
  iudea, 155, 820
Arcoleo
  Georgius, villanus, 957
  Hemanuel, de S. Lucia,
    191
  Iani, villanus, 366
arcus, 117
Ares
  Teotonicus, caporalis,
    511
Areti, 52, 732
  Fontanela, 192
  Stadhi, de ca', 93
Argeropulo
  Nicolaus, 79
Argiropulo
  Hemanuel, 643
Arianus
  Contareno of Venice, 528
Arimino
  Recardinus de, 738
Arismolus
  Contestabile equester,
    399
arma, 959, 979
Armachena
  Cherana, 948
  Maria, 316
Armachi
  Eudochia, wife of
    Theodosius, 311
  Hemanuel, 69, 317
  Marula, wife of
    Hemanuel, 69
  Theodosius, 310
armariolum, 274
Armena
  Maria, 181
Armenissa
  Cali, 770
Armicha
  Nicolaus, presbyter, 944
Armin

Çanachi, 783
  Marçoli, wife of Çanachi,
    783
  Petrus de, 46
Armino
  Cali, wife of Georgius,
    cerdo, 552
  Georgius, cerdo, 552
  N., 566
  Nicolaus, 553
  Petrus de, 305
Arminus
  Nicolaus, 149
Armolaus
  Savonaro, 619
Armorudena, 965
Arniça, 576
Arpe
  Josep de, 398
Arsenço
  Michaletus, 664
Arthire
  vinea, 388
Artimoniati
  Bartholomeus, 181
Artolina, 598
Ascolis
  Pe. de, 503
Ascolito
  Petrus de, 506
Asgurus, 520
asiole, 183, 330, 443
Asimi
  casale, 620
asolle, 788
asomato, 538
Asprocorio
  casale, 710
Asprogerena
  Cherana, 97
Astividena
  Marula, 939
Astraca
  casale, 601
Astraccus
  locus, 115
Astulfo
  Antonius, 159

Astulfus, 737
Astupaliotissa
  Biatrix, 883
Athanati
  vinea, 303
Athineo
  Herini, wife of Iani, 927
  Iani, 927
Athinea
  Eudochia, 680
Aucepis
  Anastasia, wife of
    Donatus, 163
Audochia
  Cartore called Stamurena,
    347
Augustina
  Mudacio, 337
Augustinus
  Coppo, 830
  Geço, 358, 378
  Geço of Venice, 700
  Laurencio, de, 143
Auracha
  Chomati, son of
    Sambatheus, 21
Auracoto
  locus, 350
Auradena
  calogrea, 833
Aurado
  Marcus de, aurifex, 117
Aureplasa, see Aurumplasa
aurierium, 508
aurifex
  Aurado, Marcus de, 117
  Barbafella, Georgius, 240,
    643
  Bono, Paulus, 117
  Bononia, Raphael de, 467
  Çangisti, Petrus, 613
  Cimbischi, Gulielmus, 588
  Condo, Iohannes, 466,
    501
  Dandulo, Iohannes, ex-,
    853
  Gisi, N., 541
  Gramaticopulo,

Dionissius, 807
Franciscus, 933
Habramo, Hemanuel, 16
Longo, Marinus, 67
Marcus, 504
Mauro, Iohannes, 864,
  884
Mauroceno, Marinus, 79
Petrus, 4
Pirio, Marinus, 508
Plasencia, Nicolaus de,
  322, 521
Pleiro, Marcus, 466
Rosso, Georgius, 240
Sellopulo, Georgius, 79,
  304
Theodhosius, 614
Tomasinus, 488
Trivisano, Bartholomeus,
  2
aurilortum, 29
Aurumplasa, Aurumplaxa
  Baroci, widow of Iacobus
    of Venice, 453
  Quirino, 343
  Truno, 731
auxilator
  Rosso, Leo Diesulo, 773
Avadhe
  casale, 214
Avala
  Moscana, 159
Avanante
  Corner, wife of Philipus,
    962
Avancio
  Georgius de, 507
Avancius
  Pesellis, de, 161
Avenans, see Advenans
Avini
  Georgius, 435
Avonale, 3
  Andreas, 595
  Andriola, 873
  Aniça, 390
  Antonius, 406
  Bartholomeus, 15, 593

Blasius, 307
Constancius, 865, 873
Filipa, soror, 776
Georgius, 987
Georgius, discipulus, 583
Helena, wife of Antonius,
  406
Iacobellus, 873
Iacobina, 14, 480, 603
Iacobus, 593, 594
Iohannes, 524, 534, 593,
  594
Iohannes, scriba, 548
Iulianus, 593, 594
Marçoli, daughter of
  Antonius, 407
Marcus, 5, 588, 593, 595
Maria, 595
Maria, daughter of
  Thomas, 593
Maria, wife of Nicolaus,
  marangonus, 566
Nicolaus, 792
Nicolaus, marangonus,
  566
Petrus, 221, 595, 873,
  991
Philipa, 307
Philipa, piçocara, 347
Thomas, 593, 594, 600
Thomas, son of Iulianus,
  594
Thomasina, 109, 600
Thomasina, daughter of
  Thomas, 594
Avradho
  Cali, widow of Georgius,
    277
  Georgius, 277
Axioti
  Hemanuel, 403
Aycardena, 452
Aycha, 337
  Iuliano, 186
Aymo
  Georgius, 857
  Georgius, notarius, 969
  Iohaninus, 412

Iohannes, 673, 857
Nicolaus, 74

Baboto
    Bernardus, catelanus, 625
bacalarius
    Bononia, Iacobus de,
        frater, 393
    Marcus, frater, 274
    S. Franciscus, 130
Bachino
    Nicolaus, clericus, 492
bachum, 524
bacilum, bacilus, baçilum, 9,
    529, 766
bacinelus, 9
Baçolo, 466
Baduario
    Albanus, ducha Crete, 831
    Angelus, of Venice, 398
    Petrus, ducha Crete, 205,
        291, 309, 639
Bafo, Baffo
    Andreas de Rethimo, 273
    Helena, 636
    Iohannes, 636
    Marchesina, 925
    Nicolaus, 188
    Petrus, 569
    Petrus, clericus, 568
Baiamonte
    Helena, daughter of
        Stephanus, 230
    Stephanus, 230
Baiardus
    Gradonico, 679
baiula, 314, 327, 552, 811,
    835, 959
    Aniça, 57, 366, 909
    Ana, 939
    Cali, 23, 461, 701, 909,
        931
    Caterucia, 692
    Çenser, 483
    Cherana, 54, 149
    Chieranna, 530, 576
    Frosini, 35

Herini, 337, 447, 928,
    931
Margarita, 75
Maria, 461, 571, 576,
    692, 930, 964, 974
Megallomata, Herini, 110
Moscana, 585
Paleologo, 20
Papada, 974
Sinori, Maria, 776
Soi, 257
Stamata, 905
Balaço
    Nicolaus, 236
Balarinus
    Petenario, 839
Balastrena
    Maria, 604
Balastro
    Aniça, 157, 408, 434
    Franghia, 932
    Marchesina, wife of
        Franghia, 933
    Nicholota, 576
    Periera, 26, 488, 576
    Petrus, 863
    Stamatina, daughter of
        Franghia, 932
Balbi
    Agnes, 838
    Anastassia, iudea, wife of
        Iecudha, iudeus,
        speciarius, 595
    Cataruça, daughter of
        Dardius, 247
    Chaluda, iudea, 127
    Dardius, 246
    Franciscus, 869
    Iecudha, iudeus,
        speciarius, 595
    Mariçoli, wife of Dardius,
        247
    Petrus, 246
Balbo
    Iacuda, iudeus, 127
    Iecuda, iudeus, 650
    Iohannes, 238
    Micali, iudeus, 383

Michael, 650
Sambatheus, iudeus, 595
Yeremia, iudeus, 127
Ysagia, iudeus, 127
Baldagno
    Dominicus de, presbyter,
        125
Baldu
    Agnes, 923
    Fantinus, of Venice, 897
    Marcus, 974
    Mariçoli, 888, 974
    Marinellus, son of Marcus,
        974
Balducius
    Rimano, de, 44, 59, 85
Balduin
    Iohannes, 604
Balduinus
    Signolo, 582
Baldus
    Quirino, consiliarius, 365
Balduvino
    Albanus, 41, 161, 555
    Andreas, son of Iohannes,
        555
    Balduvinus, 161
    Henrigina, wife of
        Iohannes, 160
    Iohannes, 160, 554
    Nicolaus, son of Iohannes,
        555
Balduvinus
    Balduvino, 161
    Bartholomeus, 324
balista, 9, 959
balistarius, 959
    Iohannes, famulus, 125
    Micilinus, 8
Ballarinus
    Bellinzono, de, 743
Balvina
    Pemato, de, 818
Bampaninus, Bampamius
    Quirino, 927, 977
    Quirino, son of Amoratus,
        456
bancha, 19

bancum, 9, 24, 29, 79, 98, 140, 299, 331, 414, 443, 466, 526, 637, 669, 785, 984
Bannassuta
   Pantaleo, daughter of Andreas, 271
Barandena, 916
Barastro
   Petrus, 986
   Symeon, 365
Baratius
   frater, 432
Barbadico
   Agnes, 492
   Andreas, 643, 653
   Angelus, 968, 974
   Bartholomeus, 366
   Beatrix, daughter of Bericia, 93
   Bericia, 93
   Helena, wife of Nicolaus de Venetiis, 721
   Iacobina, 586
   Iohannes, 14
   Laurencius, 637, 695, 716
   Magdalucia, widow of Michael, 973
   Marcus, 95, 196, 492, 553, 678
   Maria, 366, 716
   Mariçoli, wife of Marcus, 553
   Marinellus, son of Marcus, 492
   Marinus, 196, 492
   Nicolaus, 574, 637
   Nicolaus, de Venetiis, 721
   Pascelicena, 916
   Paulus, 684
   Philipa, wife of Iohannes, 14
   Thomas, 285, 640, 654
Barbadico Pascelicena
   Maria, 919
Barbafela
   Georgius, 428
   Georgius, aurifex, 240, 643

Nicoleta, daughter of Georgius, aurifex, 643
Nicolota, daughter of Georgius, 428
Petrus, 769
Barbara, 755, 811, 814
   Alexiopulo, daughter of Dimitrius, 940
   Çacharia, wife of Franciscus, 162
   Geno, called Pascelicena, 924
   Lambardo, 864
   Nani, de Venetiis, 829
   Trivixano, wife of Donatus de Venetiis, 618
Barbarigo
   Andreas, 412
   Iohannes, 412
   Madalucia, 888
   Michaletus, 412
Barberena, 383, 967
barberius
   Traversario, Andreas, 686
barbitonsor
   Francho, Marcus, 573
   Geno, Nicoletus, 646
   Iacobus, 573
   Vido, Nicolaus, 766
Barbo, 363
   Andreas, 75
   Barbus, 234
   Çorçi, 710
   Gabriel, 963
   Georgius, 351, 645, 665
   Hemanuel, 735
   Marchesina, 35, 457
   Marcus, 537, 583, 671
   Maria, 504
   Maria, widow of Michael, 466
   Michael, 466
   Niça, daughter of Çorçi, 710
   Nicolaus, 144
   Nicolaus, piçina, 404

Nicoletus, 671
Philipa, wife of Hemanuel, 735
Thomasina, 465
Ugolinus, 35
Barboso
   Costa, 798
barbus
   Barbo, 234
Barbuta, 130, 739
barcha, 29
Barchis
   Andreas de le, 633
Baroci, Baroçi, Barocio, Baronci, Barozi
   Agnes, wife of Iohannes, 979
   Andreas, 313, 430, 683, 713, 749, 979
   Andreas, admiratus imperii Romanie, 453, 454
   Antonia, widow of Andreas, 430
   Aureplasa, widow of Iacobus of Venice, 453
   Caterucia, 713
   Chaliça, 880
   Constancia, daughter of Marcus, 446
   Franchus, 683
   Helisera, soror, 454
   Iacobus, 749, 979
   Iacobus, de Venetiis, 453
   Iacomo, 710
   Iohannes, 104, 714, 749, 969, 978
   Marchesina, 298, 714, 749
   Marchesina, wife of Iacobus, 749
   Marcus, 445
   Marinellus, 581, 979
   Marinellus, natural son of Marcus, 446
   Marinellus, son of Andreas, 979

184
Antonius, presbyter, 696
Bartholomeus, 801
Benedicta, wife of
    Brunaurus, 179
Dinande, frater, 184
Georgius, 935
Mariçoli, 162
Nicolaus, presbyter, 273
Raphael, 184
Baxilius
    Marangelo, 155
    Marçanapulo, 253
    Marçangelo, 218
Beata
    Canale, wife of Georgius
        de, 241
    Molino, daughter of
        Leonardus, 242
    Molino, daughter of
        Marinus, 242
    Quirino, 81, 94
    Quirino, daughter of
        Georgius, 288
    Quirino, wife of
        Dominicus, 394
    Vigoncia, de, 92, 708
Beata Maria Virgo
    ecclesia, 799
    scola, 577
Beata Maria semper Virgo
    scola fratrum, 478
Beatrix, Biatrix, 430, 980
    Alexandro, wife of
        Dominicus de, 536
    Astupaliotissa, 883
    Barbadico, daughter of
        Bericia, 93
    Medio, de, 904
    Stimpalia, de, 924
    Tadhaudo, 92, 93
    Trivisano, widow of
        Dominicus, 217
Beatus Antonius
    ecclesia, 742, 746
Beatus Franciscus, 379
Beatus Gregorius, 745
Beatus Iacobus de Gallicia

ecclesia, 379
Becario
    Iohannes, 569
    Laurencius, 399
beccaria, 854
beccarius
    Iohanninus, 456
    Quirino, Leo, 655
Becheto
    Iohannes, 739
    Iohannes, comestabilis,
        pedester, 117, 868
Becontolo, see Bocontolo
Bectaro
    Iohannes, 578
Begulinus
    Francus, 416
Belacura
    Antonius, 501
    Maria, wife of Antonius,
        501
Belança
    Cherena, iudeus, wife of
        Helia, 200
    Helia, iudeus, 200
Belegno
    Chatarucia, 905
    Iohannes, 622
Belelus
    Nani, 255, 626
    Nani de Venetiis, 359
Belena
    textrix, 930
Beletus
    Gulialmo, 635
Beligno
    Caterina, 373
    Ognebene, 373
    Natalis, 327
Belilena
    Herini, 800
Belinus
    Dandulo, 389, 505
    Dandulo, Nicolaus, 258
Bella, 985
    Facadena, Thodora, 826
Bellamore
    Agnes de, 18

Andreas de, 466
Helena, widow of
    Nicolaus, 224
Iohannes de, 7, 16, 163,
    451
Laurentius de, 51, 72, 350
Nicolaus de, 224, 602
Stamatius de, 350
Belli, Beli
    Achelena, wife of
        Antonius, notarius,
        535
    Alba, wife of Antonius,
        99
    Alisa, daughter of
        Nicoletus, 488
    Angelus, 509
    Antonius, 99, 288
    Antonius, notarius, 535
    Franciscus, 169
    Helena, wife of Antonius,
        99
    Iacobus, 186
    Iohannes, 7, 11
    Iohannes, notarius,
        presbyter, capellanus
        duche Crete, 511
    Marchesina, wife of
        Nicolaus, 626
    Marinus, 509
    Nicolaus, 185, 186, 255,
        626
    Nicoletus, 488
    Petrus, 185
    Thomasina, 571
    Thomasina, vetula, 924
Bellinus, Belignus
    Dandulo, 633
    Dandulo, Nicolaus, 201
Bellinzono
    Ballarino de, 743
Bello
    Nicoletus, 465
Bellono
    Dominicus, 346, 357, 360
    Dominicus, scriba palatii,
        341
    Georgius, 315, 318

Mussule, 190
Ranerio, de, 423
Rippa, de, 215
Rippa, de, magister, 662
Riva, de, 64
Simiteculo, 5, 613
Venerio, 338
Vonal, 855
Blico
Michael, 318
Blonda, 509
Popo, 478
Blunda
Foscareno, wife of
Claretus, 264
Boali, see Bualli
bobiceum, 649
Bocanigra
Andreas, peliparius, 404
Iohannes, 34
Bocasso
Antonius, 193
bochetum perlarum, 916
Boçia
Helena, 140
boçolo, boçolum, 526, 599
Bocontolo, Bocuntolo
Agnes, 844
Agnes, wife of Marcus,
181
Amoretus, 41
Angelus, 863
Aniça, 39
Dominicus, 109, 774, 778,
786
Dominicus, scribanus, 183
Hergina, 632
Ia., 632
Iacobina, 863
Iacobus, 56, 388, 781

M., 632
Marcus, 34, 36, 38, 40,
41, 181, 305
Marinus, presbyter, 93,
671
Philipus, 632, 844
Bogtolo

Martinus, presbyter, 627
Boiardis
Bonafacius de, of
Ruberio, comestabilis
equester, 511
Cinellus de, of Ruberio,
512
Boldu
Agnes, widow of Marcus,
of Venice, 929
Fantinus, 914
Marcus, de Venetiis, 929
Bollani, Bollan
Andreas, 103, 898, 939
Çanachius, 717
Franciscus, de Venetiis,
843
Georgius, 867, 883
Iacobus, 35, 102
Iohannes, 12
Marçoli, 35
Marieta, wife of
Franciscus, de
Venetiis, 843
Marchesina, 898
Mariçoli, wife of
Andreas, 898
Marula, wife of Thomas,
717
Nicolaus, 102
Nicoletus, natural son of
Thomas, 717
Palma, 102
Thomas, 102, 717
Tomas, 35
Bolgaro
Vituri, 896
Bombea
casale, 757
Bona, 15, 37, 90, 95, 618
Garçetena, 413
Rimano, daughter of
Maximus de, 44
soror, 342, 909
widow of Pilatus, 149
Bonacorsso
Michael, 942
Bonacursius

Brancha, caporalis
pedester, 129
Cremona, de, 55
Fregona, de, magister,
644, 652
Grimani, 966
Toscano, 299
Bonafacius
Boiardis, de, de Ruberio,
comestabilis
equester, 511
Vigoncia, de, 632
Bonafans, Bonafanta, 185
Geno, wife of Matheus,
20, 547
Trun, wife of
Bartholomeus, 376
Bonafemena
Venerio, wife of Petrus,
536
Bonaldis, Bonaudis
Iohannes de, magister,
cirurgicus, 195, 203,
265, 662
Bonamico
Nicoleta, 887
Bonasegna
frater, 909
Bonaspeçilança, 76
Bonasudhus
Stanchario, de, 400
Bonasvita, 419
Bonaventurosa, 557
Boneta
Albi, daughter of
Nicolaus, 600
Bonfanta, 185
Bonfilio
Bortolomeus de, gastalde,
106
Maria de, 342
Boni
casale, 221
Georgius, 881
Bonifacio
Sofia de, 984
Bonifacium
castrum, 162, 392

Bonifacius
 Trivisano, sutor, 534
Bonivento
 Iacobus de, magister,
  medicus, cirurgicus,
  968
Bonmarcadho
 Marchesina de, 73
Bono
 Agnes, 23
 Agnes, widow of
  Nicolaus, 279
 Alexander, de Venetiis,
  897
 Andreas, 71
 Antonius, 230
 Bartholomeus, 149, 445,
  614, 818, 926
 calogrea, da cha', 909
 Costas, 40
 Dominicus, 296, 431
 Dominicus, ducha Crete,
  953
 Dominicus, son of
  Stephanus, notarius,
  543
 Felix, 92
 Francischina, daughter of
  Stephanus, notarius,
  543
 Georgius, 711
 Helena, 21, 36
 Helena, daughter of
  Petrus, 327
 Helena, wife of Nicolaus,
  640, 654
 Hemanuel, 926, 947
 Herigina, natural daughter
  of Iacobus, 37
 Iacoba, widow of
  Laurencius, 855
 Iacobina, 927
 Iacobina, wife of
  Bartholomeus, 818
 Iacobinus, 690, 732
 Iacumicius, 731
 Iohannes, 36, 71, 100,
  376, 487, 683, 718,

732, 927
 Iohannes, notarius, 196
 Laurencius, 855
 Magdalena, widow of
  Nicolaus, 963
 Marcocia, 259
 Marcus, buticlarius, 722
 Margarita, 839
 Maria, 36
 Mariçoli, 927, 939
 Moscana, 677
 N., 550
 Nicolaus, 279, 498, 540,
  545, 549, 559, 640,
  654, 927, 937, 963
 Nicolaus, discipulus, 525,
  533, 538, 541, 554
 Nicolaus parvus, 601
 Nicolaus, son of
  Stephanus, 519
 Nicoletus, 536
 Nicoletus, parvus, 596
 Pascalis, 607, 608
 Pascalius, 572
 Pasqualis, 335
 Paulus, aurifex, 117
 Peria, 36
 Peria, widow of Petrus,
  20
 Petrus, 20, 327, 947, 953
 Petrus, son of Stephanus,
  notarius, 543
 Philipus, buticlarius, 622
 Placencia, 230, 682
 Pothiti, daughter of
  Stephanus, notarius,
  543
 Sophia, wife of Philipus,
  buticlarius, 622
 Sta., 880
 Stamatius, 885
 Stamatus, 890
 Stephanus, 431, 519
 Stephanus, notarius, 446,
  543
 Theostictus, penitencialis
  monasterium SS
  Apostolorum, 784

Thomasina, wife of
 Iohannes, 100
Bonohomo
 Marcus de, 408
 Marudalena, widow of
  Marcus, 408
Bononia, 737
 Andreas de, frater, prior,
  393
 Bartholomeus de, 117
 Bonovicinus de, 711
 Burin, Iacobus,
  speciarius, son of
  Iohannes, de, 393
 Gerardus de, frater, 85
 Iacobus de, frater,
  bacalarus, 393
 Raphael de, aurifex, 467
 Stephanus de, 191
 Surfiis, Tadeus de, de,
  394
 Tomaxio de, maistro, 989
 Vedoacis, Thomas de,
  notarius, de, 393
 Venturinus de, 711
 Zigerdoti, Philipus, de,
  393
Bonsignor
 Antonius de, 620
 Bartholomeus de, 159
 Nicolaus, 949
 Philipa, 939
 Robertus de, 121
Bonsolo, Bonsollo
 Iohannes, 318, 450
Bonovicinus
 Bononia, de, 711
Bonsignore
 Costa de, 715
Bonuça
 Gisi, wife of Philipus,
  317
Bonus Iohannes
 Caurolis, de, 96
 Padua, de, 64, 199
Bonvicina
 Helena, 184
Bonzuora

Çambono, wife of
Nasimbene, 862
bordonarius
Georgius, slave, 447
Michael, 107
Theodorus, 183
Borgno
Cristoforus de, 867
Margarita, wife of
Cristoforus de, 867
Borgognono
Angelus, 964, 969
Iacobina, 963
Bornio
Christoforus de, 117
Borocio
Andreas, 154
Helena, widow of
Andreas, 154
Bortalio, 962
Bortolameo, see Bartholomeus
Bortolamio, see
Bartholomeus
bos, 214, 287, 600, 965
Bosolina
monacha, 633
Bossulina
monaca, 233
Botafocho
Stefanus, notarius, 120
botonus, 974
bote, 330
Botheta, 447
botonus, 172, 535
braçali, 130
braçalini, 394
Braçamonte
Iohannes, presbyter, 411,
547, 548
Braçodoro
Dominicus, presbyter, 414
Braçole
Albertinus, 652
Bradiolo
Iohannes, 257
Bragadino
Antonia, daughter of
Michaletus, 661

Brandinus, son of
Michaletus, 661
Francischina, daughter of
Michaletus, 661
Marchesina, daughter of
Michaletus, 661
Marinus, 661
Michaletus, of Venice,
661
Neapolion, son of
Michaletus, 661
Stephanus, 661
Bragadinus
Bragadino, son of
Michaletus, 661
Brancha
Bonacursius, caporalis
pedester, 129
Iacobus de la, 399
Branchio
iudeus, 120
Bresano
Antonius, clericus, 664
Bresiadheno
Herini, 39
Bretenorio
Nicolaus de, 738
breviarium, 273, 664
Brexan, see Brexiano
Brexiano, Brixiano
Agnes, 81, 494
Andreas, 51
Andreas, notarius, 49, 279
Antonius, 63, 215, 411,
685
Antonius, presbyter, 274,
494, 677
Beneventus, 560
Benevenutus, son of
Nicolaus, 47, 51, 798
Bartholomeus, 437
Bartholomeus, peliparius,
404
Bn., 577
Caterina, 353, 391
Franciscus, peliparius,
son of Bartholomeus,
437

Guiellmus, peliparius,
494
Ianachius, peliparius, 494
Iohannes, presbyter, 28
Marçoli, 105
Maria, wife of Nicolaus,
151
Maria, wife of Nicolaus,
notarius, 47
N., 543
Nicolaus, 43, 51, 55, 66,
151, 540, 551, 565,
579, 767
Nicolaus, notarius, 47
Nicoleta, 912
Nicoletus, 767
Nicolota, widow of
Bartholomeus, 437
Paulus, 912
Petrus, 484
Phylippa, 51
senior, 409
brigata carnisprivii, 743
brigesia, 90
Briola
Peradiso, 878
Brioli
Betto, 899
Brisiano
Antonio, pre, 896
Brixia
Francus de, soldatus, 400
Brogodino
Marcus, 615
Brogognessa, 288
Maria, 692
Brogognono
Angelus, 252
Angelus, son of Marcus,
342
Iacobina, wife of Marcus,
342
Iacobus, 287
Kirulus, son of Marcus,
342
Marcus, 342
Maria, 224
Maria tu, 920

Petrus, 342
Petrus, riparius, 279
Brogognosa
pauper, 714
Brogondione
Caterinus, 610
Constantia, wife of
Iohannes, 609
Iohannes, 609
Leo, famulus, 689
Marcus, 62, 609
Maria, 609
Marula, 927
Nicoletus, 610
Brois
Ianulli, 659
Bruçeseno
Caterina, 920
Brucesia
Çironda, 544
Brugondione
Angelus, 539
Brun
Agnes, 857
Brunaurus
Baxilio, 179
Brundusio
Pignatellus, Nicolaus,
magister, de, 805
Brunelo
Costas, villanus, 876
Petrus, 12
Seni, wife of Petrus, 12
Bruno
Alvirandus, 774
Gulielmus, 58
Iohannes, 774, 778
Oliverus, 778
Buaeda
piliçaria, 380
Buali, Boalli
Taliapetra, Petrus, 352,
388
Buça
Iacomina, 83
buculerium, 711
Bufo
Petrus, clericus, 847

bulgara
Cali, 712
Cali, slave, 370
Greco, Maria, 856
Maria, 753
Maria, slave, 473, 488,
683, 695, 987, 990
bulgarus
Dimitri, slave, 370
Georgius, slave, 968
Michael, slave, 298
slave, 370
Burgundione
Agnes, widow of Iacobus,
515
Iacobus, 515
Iohannes, 515
Iohannes, son of Petrus,
515
Mariçoli, natural daughter
of Marcus, 515
Petrus, 515
Burgondrone
Marula, sister of Petrus,
preco, 49
Petrus, preco, 49
Burtino
Baselius, 649
Busignore
Pasqualis, de, 128
buticlarius, butiglarius
Antonius, 498
Bono, Marcus, 722
Bono, Philipus, 622
Georgius, 233
Iohannes, 298
Ialina, Michael, 248
butiglarius, see Buticlarius

Çabela
Stamatius, 950
Caçamba
casale, 951
Pachi, Nicolaus, de, 966
Cabriel
Çacharia, de Venetiis, 914
cacabum, 9

Çacha
Casani, iudeus, 988
iudeus, 300, 301
Çacharia, 498
Barbara, wife of
Franciscus, 162, 288
Cabriel, 914
Franciscus, 162, 196
Muturia, de, 64
Vendelino, 592
Vindilino, 90, 269, 515
Çachariadena
Marula, 939
Çachetus
Sclavo, 287, 482, 630
Çachonissa, 514
Çachus
papas, 773
cacia, 393
Cacilidhi, 601
Çaco, Caco
Anna, santula, 928
Antonius, son of
Dimitrius, 918
Chali, daughter of
Dimitrius, 918
Çorçi, 962
Dimitrius, 918
Georgius, 918, 923
Georgius, son of
Dimitrius, 918
Margarita, 919, 920, 928
Nicolaus, papas, 695
Caçochorio
Iohannes, 168
cacoga, 459
Caçomata
Saclicchi, Georgius,
called, 596
Çaconia
Franciscus de, called
Georgius, slave, 274
caçoprina, 108
Caçulena
Eudochia, 845
Caçunu
Theodora, 149
Cacura

Calogeropulo, wife of
Leo, 866
Calomendrino, natural
daughter of Iohannes,
48
Candida, de, 121
Carpathea, nena, 679, 972
Cartero, daughter of
Thomas, 826
Chandachyti, widow of
Iohannes, 296
Charandina, 550
Charcomata, daughter of
Michael, 254
Colla de, marescalcus, 738
Contareno, widow of
Arianus of Venice,
528
Cornario, wife of
Iohannes, 788
Çuliadena, 636
Cursari, daughter of
Hemanuel, 822
Damiano, wife of
Michatius, 690
Danese, 113
Deso, widow of Marcus,
406
Diminiti, widow of Lucas,
311
Dochanos, wife of
Michael, 522
Dono, 802
ex-slave, 533, 619, 620,
835, 859, 921
famula, 811, 818
Filomatena 768
Folisso, widow of
Laurencius, 534
Forciano, 242
Forcianudena, 374
Fovea, widow of Petrus,
522
Fussudena, 768
Gavrilena, 758
Gisi, 766
Gisi, wife of Theodorus,
ex-slave, 286

Gligoropulo, daughter of
Nicolaus, 685
Gradonico, natural
daughter of
Bertucius, 823
Gradonico, widow of
Nicolaus, 11
Gripiotissa, 452, 818
Guernioti, widow of
Georgius, 604
Guverotena, 589
Habramo, wife of
Hemanuel, aurifex,
16
iudea, 127, 323, 445, 450,
460, 639, 642, 653,
892, 954
Leo, iudeus, 458
Leo, iudeus, son of
Moyses, 459
Linadhena, iudea, wife of
Moyses, iudeus, 459
Liveri, wife of Georgius,
corrigarius, 213
Luchidhena, 140
Lumbardo, wife of
Georgius, 320
Maçamurdi, natural
daughter of
Michali, 19
Macrea, 347
Magistropiero, wife of
Marinus, called
Vasmulo, 516
Malacenti, 576
Manolicena, 956, 991
Manolu, 974
Martuça, widow of
Hemanuel, 788
Marulu, 107, 716
Matheo, tu, 701
Mercato, wife of
Theodorus, 114
Metachieristi, 588
Moyses, iudeus, son of
Leo, 458
Milea, 321
Monomati, daughter of

Costas, 386
Mothono, de, 147
Mucio, 48
Mulino, natural daughter
of Marcus, 758
Musalo, venderigola, 395
Mudaço, tu, 706
nena, 37, 461, 931
Nomico, daughter of
Samuel, 123
Orso, wife of Philipus,
527
Papadhia S. Dimitri, 296
Paramandi, wife of
Michael, 658
Pastela, wife of
Lingiacus, 246
Pateremuchena, 590
Paulopulo, ex-slave, 735
Pefani, daughter of
Costas, 40
Pelecano, wife of
Matheus, 912
Penindarena, 737
Perdhicarena, 74
Perdicari, monaca, widow
of Georgius, 214
Petronicola, daughter of
Costas, 533
Piçocara, 262
Placentia, widow of
Petrus de, 374
Plati, tu, 49, 283
Politissa, 833
Portu, de, ex-slave, 692
Pronicadhena, 784
Quirino, de ca', now
Catafigi, monaca,
140
Quirino, daughter of
Manoli, 86
Rapani, widow of
Theodorus, 640, 654
Riço, daughter of
Nicolaus de, 16
Rimano, mother of
Balducius, 85
Rosso, 717

Ruzerena, 732
Saligardena, 778
Samerya, tu, iudea, 892
Santurnea, 94
Saracenus, daughter of
Iohannes, 141
Sarnudi, 508
Savonario, 895
Sclavo, 129
Scordili, daughter of Sifi,
928
serviciale, 116
servitrix, 46, 466, 503,
956
Sestofolena, 50
Siligardo, natural daughter
of Petrus, 539
slave, 28, 68, 72, 86, 100,
103, 122, 224, 230,
250, 284, 287, 343,
363, 364, 383, 395,
427, 431, 536, 582,
629, 636, 782, 794,
875, 904, 909, 883,
894
Stathi, 647
Staurachena, 990
Staurachi, 397
Stratigu, 908
Suriano, wife of Calo, 197
Suriano, wife of Iohannes
called Capelus, 601
Tornichio, widow of
papas Michael, 769
Trivixano, wife of
Tomasinus, 147
Turadena, 705
Turco, wife of Petrus, 149
turca, slave, 599
Venerio, wife of Michael,
466
Vido, widow of Nicolaus,
barbitonsor, 766
Vigonçia, de, 933
visastra, 431
Vitalis, wife of Costa,
incantator, 577
vlacha, ex-slave, 337

Vlasto, wife of
Constantinus, 108
Xeriti, wife of Georgius,
caligarius, 337
Xilea, 508
Yncreseçina, 778
Zavuchena, 869
caliarus, 540
Calica, Caliça, Calicia,
Chalicia, 250, 324, 559,
675, 764, 944
Andreas, 717
Antonius, 749
Baroci, 880
Comita, daughter of
Nicolaus, frenarius,
149
Cremona, daughter of
Frangulus de, 814
famula, 746
Foscari, natural daughter
of Marchesinus, 296
Fosculo, 170
Maça, 838
Marino, daughter of
Iacobus, 771
Mauro, daughter of
Iohannes, 108
Molino, natural daughter
of Marcus de, 714
Paganuço, wife of Petrus,
184
Raguseo, wife of Marcus,
168
Sclavo, 849
servicialis, 812
slave, 271, 814
Tricha, daughter of Iani,
papas, 591
Caliceni, 257
Calicha
M., 494
Calicia, 573, 624, 649, 673
Staurachi, 395
Calicoca, 452
caliga, 130
caligaria, 959
Venetanda, 380

caligarius, 756
Capaci, Marcus, 5
Cirita, Antonius, 50
Frangulus, 787
Mengalo, Nicolaus, 1
Michale, 678
Mundeo, Nicolaus de, 6
Nigroponte, Hemanuel
de, 775
Trivixano, Frangulus, 787
Caligopulo
Maria, widow of Thomas,
242
Nicolaus, 434
Thomas, 242
Calimnea
Maria, 74
Calimneadhena, 250
Herini, 296
Calinichi
Paradiso, monacha, 771
Samea, monacha, 181
Calisa, 400
Caliso
nena, 383
Caliva
casale, 601
Iohannes, 84, 619
Nicolaus, 474, 523, 619
Petrus, 976
calix, 233, 428, 909
Callenas, 944
Callopulo
Iohannes, papas, 955
Callus, 10
Musselle, 802
Calo
iudeus, 821
Marinus, calogrea, 884
Suriano, 197
villanus, 397
Caloçesa
Doto, 317
Calogalo
Iacobina, 873
Calogerico
casale, 161
Calogeropulo

Chali, wife of Leo, 866
Leo, 866
Calogerus, calogero
    Andrinopoliti, Nicolaus,
      984
    Castamoniti, Nicolaus,
      papas, of Rethimno,
      925
    Chefala, 965, 980
    Chortacenus, 552
    Çorçi, 362
    Gavra, Matheus, papas,
      680
    Grimano, papas, Chefala,
      908
    Gulambe, Georgius, 799
    Iohanachi, 824
    Lano, 949
    Marcus, papas, 681
    Mauro, 720
    Mengolo, Georgius, 849
    Michale, 678
    Mileo, Marcus, 691
    Orbo, 984
    Selopulo, Giorgici, 982
    S. Constantinus, 992
    S. Iohannes Theologus,
      980
    Theostioctui, confessor SS
      Apostolorum, 949
    Theostirictus,
      pneumaticus, 708
    Thocaropulo, Petrofani,
      845
    Yeosiph, papas, 849
Calognomo
    Georgius, called Cutrulli,
      397
calogrea, 552, 946, 985
    Alissafi, 341
    Angelu, 970
    Auradena, 833
    Bono, de cha', 909
    Carandino, 882
    Chastarena, Luludhia, 772
    Cherana, 970
    Cherana, ex-slave, 984
    Chrussi, 984

Clinathati, 814
Cufoplectu, Catafigi, 766
Eudochia, nena, 965
Eufemia, 925
Eugenia, 692
Franguli, 928
Helena, 411
Helena, daughter of Pasia
    Sancti, 415
Herini, diaconissa, 351
Ligandena, 851
Magdalena, 859
Magdalini, 708
Maria, slave, 343
Miradhia, 949
Misinena, Chalinichi, 832
nena, 710
Paramadena, 950
Pitharullena, Maricioli,
    746
Rodhiani, 542
Sclavena, 347
Sclavo, Sifiossini, widow
    of Nicolaus,
    murarius, 768
Sitiacudena, 856
Soticli, 849
Taneligena, 542
Theodulli, 806
Theofilopulo, Maria, 689
Theostireti, 947
turcha, nena, 347
Calomati
    Michael, 74, 987
Calomendrino
    Cali, natural daughter of
      Iohannes, 48
    Iohannes, 48
Çalon
    Antonius, Lamber, 320
Calona
    Nichitas, 287
    Vasilius, 29
Calopti
    Georgius, papas, 603
Calos
    Mussulo, 56, 101
Calotherina, 23

Calothetina
    Herini, 920
Calu
    casale, 154
Caluci, 629
    Aniça, daughter of
      Nicolaus, 630
    Nicolaus, 630
Caluda, Caludia
    Chomati, wife of
      Auracha, son of
      Sambatheus, 22
    Balbi, iudea, 127
    iudea, 127
Caludena, 283
Calumeadhena
    Herini, 314
Caluna
    Petrus, 189
Çamano
    Nicolaus, 176, 309
Camariano
    Hemanuel, 503
Çamatena
    iudea, 552
Cambaluri
    Efdhoquia, daughter of
      Iohannes, 632
    Iohannes, 632
Cambanellus, 643
Çambela, Çambella
    Andreas, 688, 767, 768,
      771, 773, 775, 779,
      782, 784, 785, 789
    Stimpalia, de, 700
Çambi
    Costas, 98
Cambia, 527
Çambono
    Bonzuora, wife of
      Nasimbene de, 862
    Nasimbene de, 862
Cambonus
    Marcus, presbyter,
      capellanus, 316
camera Crete, 831
camera imprestitorum, 763
camerarius Comunis, 305

Cametena, 705
Camici
  Dominicus, frater, 557
Campagnola
  Quirino, 347
  Quirino, widow of
    Andreas, 234
Campana
  Antonius de la,
    stipendiarius, 831
Çampanena
  Potha, 992
Çampani, 196
  Agnes, natural daughter of
    Petrus, 294
  Cecilia, 488
  cha', 963
  Franciscus, 294, 488
  Iacobus, 902
  Iohannes, 293, 294
  Marchesina, wife of
    Petrus, 293
  Marinus, 294
  Nicolaus, son of Petrus,
    294
  Pauleta, daughter of
    Franciscus, 488
  Petrus, 293, 329
Camulo
  Georgius, preco, 948
Çamus
  Iacobus, 419
Çana
  Vicença, da', 994
Çanachius, Çananchi, 782
  Armin, 783
  Dono, 796
  Fermo, da, noder, 783
  Geno, 795
  Gradonico, 941
  Mesina, de, 832
  Plachina, 934
  Portu, de, cerdo, 882
  Taliapera, 920
  Traversario, 921
  Vigonça, de, 826, 934
  Ystrego, 931
Canale, Canal

Andriolo da, 905
Antonius de, 109, 301,
  810, 968, 986
Bartholomeus de, 170
Beata, wife of Georgius
  de, 241
Eufrossinus de, 288
F. de, 648
Fontana, widow of
  Antonius de, 810
Francisca, wife of Marcus
  de, 176, 287
Francischina, daughter of
  Nicolo da, 390
Georgius de, 241, 286
Guido de, 190
Hemanuel de, 527, 605
Iohannes de, 109, 139,
  169, 287
Iordanus de, 287, 288
Leonardus de, 269, 320
Magdalena de, 519
Marchesina, widow of
  Marinus de, 346
Marcus de, 18, 176, 286,
  377, 499
Marcus, son of Iordanus
  de, 288
Mariçoli, wife of
  Iohannes de, 139
Marinus de, 170, 346
Marula, daughter of
  Georgius de, 242
Marula, daughter of
  Nicolo da, 390
Nicolaus de, 101, 170,
  201, 206, 258, 287,
  811
Nicolo da, 390
Petrus de, 301
Potha, widow of
  Hemanuel de, 527,
  605
Rosa, natural daughter of
  Marcus de, 287
Stephano da, 905
Theodorus de, 736
Vi. de, 643, 653

Canali
  Antonius de, 166
  Petrus de, 166
  Petrus de, supercomitus,
    831
Canalo
  Iohannes, 37
Canani
  Hemanuel, 942
Çanbon
  Marinus, 441
  Marinus, sellarius, frater
    scole S. Marie
    Cruciferorum, 441
Çancarolo, Çancaruolo
  Iacobus, 74, 668, 794
  Iohannes, 140, 538, 585,
    601, 606
  Leo, 979
  Marinus, widow of
    Nicolaus, 538
  Nicolaus, 538
cancellarius
  Parma, Michael de, 906
cancellarius Crete
  Firmo, Andreas de, 53,
    60, 68, 69, 198, 272,
    610, 644, 651-653,
    655-660, 662
  Grimani, Dominicus,
    notarius, 952, 953,
    960, 993
cancellarius Rethimni
  Morgano, Iohannes,
    notarius, 994
cancellarius Sithie
  Morgano, Iohannes, 976
Çancharole, see Çancarolo
candela ceree batutis, 880
Candelorus
  Donçorçi, son of
    Nicolaus, 764
Candaquiti, see Chandachiti
candhyanus
  Orso, Nicolaus, presbyter,
    papatu, 417
Candida
  Cali de, 121

Marinus de, frater, 37
Petrus de, 252
Çane, 962
Aniça, widow of Petrus,
da Mantoa, spatarius,
805, 807
Antonius, son of Petrus,
da Mantoa, spatarius,
805
Loredani, 905
Blança, 986
Çaneta, soror, daughter of
Nicolaus, 993
Catarucia, 255
Franciscus, 255
Iohannes, 993
Marina, wife of Nicolaus,
993
Marinus, 995
Nicolaus, 255, 993
Nicolaus, called Pançono,
of Venice, 254
Petrus, da Mantoa,
spatarius, 804, 807
Philipus, of Venice, 254
Thomas, 254
Zacharias, 995
Çanelus, 181
Çaneta
Çane, soror, daughter of
Nicolaus, 993
Çordano, wife of Iohannes
of Venice, coraçanus,
935
Cordeferro, sister of
Iohannes, 25
Pellossa, 931
Piloso, widow of Marcus,
242
Rippa, wife of
Bartholomeus de, 193
Caneveta, 408
Çangari
Helena, femina, daughter
of Michael, 316
Michael, 316
Çangarino
Maria, 542

Çangaropulo
Iohannes, called
Condoiani, 435
Çangisti
Agnes, wife of Petrus,
aurifex, 613
Marizoli, daughter of
Petrus, aurifex, 614
Petrus, aurifex, 613
Çangola, 526, 548
Canea, see Chanea
Çani
Moresini, 905
Çanicha
Quirino, 709
Çanin
Pasqualigo, son of
Iacobus, of Venice,
994
Çanina, 108, 405, 468, 490,
530, 869, 976
Canale, widow of
Leonardus de, 269
Curtessi, 972
Matherelo, wife of
Bertucius of Venice,
531
Signolo, 582
Valaresso, 923, 930
Venerio, 284
Çanini
Marcello, 716
Çaninus, 835
Foscareno, 974
Manolesso, 880
Mendrino, 691
Michael, 959
Papadopulo, 987
Quirino, 798
Steno, 898
Vigonçia, de, 933
Caniotissa
Xeni, 826
canipa, 274, 353
caniparia, 801
Canis
Iohannes, 43
canonicus Archadiensis

Mudacio, Ludas,
presbyter, 442
canonicus Calamonens
Raynerio, Iacob de, 616
canonicus Gerapetrensis
Fuschi, Andreas,
presbyter,
archidiaconus, 663
Çanpari
Georgius, faber, 426
Margarita, wife of
Georgius, faber, 426
Cantela
Nicolaus, peliparius, 404
cantor Cretensis
Rubri, Iacobus, presbyter,
412
cantor ecclesie Crete
Caucho, Georgius,
presbyter, 858
cantor S. Tito
Antonius, presbyter, 273
Capaci
Herini, 6
Marcus, caligarius, 5
Maria, sister of Marcus, 6
Marinus, 6
Capacino
Herini, wife of Petrus,
534
Capadhoca, Capadoca
Andreas, 10
Andreas, papas, 891
Maria, widow of papas
Hemanuel, 10
Micale, papas, 784
Çapani
Franciscus, 159
Herini, widow of
Franciscus, 159
Çaparino
Manfredus, frater, 687
capassa, 287
capedale, 330
Capelario
Antonius, son of
Stephanus, 617
Maria, wife of Stephanus,

616
Nicolaus, son of
Stephanus, 617
Philipa, daughter of
Stephanus, 617
Stephanus, 616
Zanachius, son of
Stephanus, 617
Capella
Daniel, 951
Iohannes, papas, 769
Thomas, 935, 936
capellanus
Basilius, presbyter, S.
Tito, 343
Cambonus, Marcus,
presbyter, 316
Michael, frater, 162
Michael, presbyter, 603
Nicolaus, prebyter, 519
Nigroponte, Iohannes de,
presbyter, 195, 664
Yspania, Michael de,
frater, 593, 595
capellanus Castri Belvidere
Nicolaus, presbyter, 402
capellanus cretensis
Nigroponte, Iohannes de,
presbyter, 408
capellanus duche Crete
Belli, Iohannes, presbyter,
notarius, 511
capellanus ecclesie Crete
Dandulo, Petrus,
presbyter, 428
capellanus S. Tito
Firmo, Iacobus de,
presbyter, 54
Floravans, presbyter, 548
Nicolaus, presbyter, 547
Nicolicius, presbyter, 544
Capello
Ieronimus, 804
Iohannes, consilarius, 123
Nicoletus, 668
Philipus, 668, 962
Capelus
Suriano, Iohannes, called,

601
capiçale, 9, 568
capicium, 69
Capistri
cavalleria, 339
Capitalo
Iohannes, mensurator,
374
capitaneus Crete
Mauroceno, Lodovicus,
762
capitaneus generalis Crete
Venerio, Antonius, 906
capitergium, 502
capitulum Grecum, 538
Caporalis
Ares, teotonicus, 511
Scarsellis, Iohannes de,
de Florentia, 738
caporalis equester
Florencia, Iohannes de,
130
caporalis pedester
Brancha, Bonacursius,
130
cappa, 738, 806
capreta, 435
capsa, 9, 29, 494, 523, 526,
548, 751, 868, 959
Capsale, 22, 498, 587
iudeus, 459
capsela, 24, 26, 79, 140, 244,
556, 678, 684, 773, 784
Capselario
Georgius, 148
capsula, 422, 466
capuceum, 937
Capuço
Helena, wife of Iohannes,
268
Iohannes, 268
capucium, 130, 756
capud, 383
capudtergium, 318
Capulus
iudeus, 988
caputhum, 273
caputogium, 173

Cara, 606
Çara
Piero de, 905
Caracausa, 151
Carandina
Cali, 550
Herini, 550
Carandino
Alexius, 48
Aniça, wife of Michael,
237
chalogrea, 882
Honesta, wife of
Nicolaus, 889
Iohannes, 628
Michael, 237
Nicolaus, 791, 889
Vasmulo tu, Christina,
856
Çarapti, 90
Carasa
Georgius, 122
Iohannes, 122
Maria, wife of Vasilius,
122
Michael, 122
Nicolaus, 122
Vasilius, 122
Caravella, Caravello
Agnes, 409
Agnes, daughter of
Iacobus, 418
Agnes, daughter of
Michael, 250
Agnes, widow of Iacobus,
271
Agnes, wife of Iacobus,
629
Anastassu, widow of
Nicolaus, 18
Andreas, natural son of
Franciscus, 369
Angelia, 259
Angelus, 84, 196, 473,
630
Angelus, 259
Antonius, 895
Bartholomeus, 461

Castelana
  Venetiis, de, 265
castellanus
  Dema, Ravichus, 120
Castelle
  Franciscus da le,
    comestabilis, 511
Castelo
  Gulielmus de, frater, 408
Castro
  Raymundus de, presbyter,
    819
Castrofilacha
  Dominicus, 851
  Georgius, 852
  Iohannes, 852
  Marula, wife of
    Dominicus, 851
castrum
  Belvidere, 206
  Bonifacium, 162, 392, 402
  Millepotami, 307
  Mirabellum, 369, 831
  Ricele, 121
  Sithia, 902
  Tegmali, 227
  Tocella, 120
Catacalo
  Gabriel, 846
Catafigi
  Cufoplectu, calogrea, 766
  monacha, 804
Catalacteno
  Angelina, 39
Catalagari
  casale, 799
catalagrum, 564
Catalgieno
  Aniça, 552
Catamano
  Michael, papas, 517
Catania
  Petrus de, specialis, 785
Cataruça, Catarucia, 414, 531,
  634, 743, 761, 763, 903
  baiula, 692
  Balbi, daughter of Darius,
    247

Baroci, 713
Belegno, 905
Biaqua, soror, 675
Çane, 255
ex-slave, 845
Fino, 762
Foscareno, daughter of
  Marinus, 264
Madio, daughter of
  Nicolaus de, de
  Venetiis, 872
Mauro, wife of Thomas,
  de Venetiis, 855
Mauroceno, daughter of
  Michaletus, 356
Pasqualigo, wife of
  Catarucia, 687
Quirino, 838
Catarinus, 225, 283, 427
  Ialina, 207, 228
Catarucia, Cataruça
  Çote, daughter of
    Nicoletus, de
    Venetiis, 409
  Macharelo, natural
    daughter of Rigucius,
    568
  Mauroceno, 379
  Venier, 338
Çate
  Laurentius, 380
  Maria, wife of Laurentius,
    380
Catellan
  Dimitrius, 131
  Donata, wife of Nicolaus,
    peliparius, 440
  Marcioli, 845
  Marcus, frater, 440
  Nicolaus, peliparius, 440
  Zanina, daughter of
    Dimitrius, 131
Catellana
  Sophia, 131
Catellani, 208
Catellano
  Andreas, 287, 330
  Benedictus, 711

Bernardus, 527, 712, 713
Frangulla, 330
Frangullus, 481, 604, 666
Guillialminus, natural son
  of Iohannes, custos,
  518
Helena, 666
Iacobina, 635
Iohannes, custos, 518
Marcus, frater, 273
Maria, daughter of
  Frangulus, 604
Maria, wife of
  Frangullus, 481
Nicolaus, 273
Petrus, 712, 713, 960
catellanus
  Baboto, Bernardus, 625
  Gorgorapti, Hemanuel,
    called, 159
  Helia, iudeus, 820
  Sascaes, Gulialmus, 625
Caterina, 115, 234, 319, 380,
  411, 419, 542, 640, 654,
  740, 883
  Anaplioti, daughter of
    Leo, 774
  Ancona, de, 242
  Beligno, 373
  Blasii, wife of Blasius,
    105
  Brexan, 391
  Brixiano, 353
  Bruçeseno, 920
  Calbo, widow of
    Antonius, 164
  Cavisino, 716
  Cordeferro, wife of
    Rogerius, 24
  Dandulo, daughter of
    Belinus, 505
  ex-serviciale, 901
  Ferraria, wife of Michael
    de, 381
  Firmo, natural daughter
    of Antonius de, 60
  Firmo, daughter of
    Franciscus de, 67

Cerca
  Nicolaus, 12
  Seni, daughter of
    Nicolaus, 12
cerdo
  Armino, Georgius, 552
  Baroçi, Nicolaus, 517
  Charchopulo, Georgius,
    902
  Flabia, Iacobus, 91
  Iustiniano, Basilius, 908
  Maestropiero, Iohannes,
    501
  Mussuro, Iohannes, 713
  Pascaligo, Georgius, 907
  Paulus, 117
  Piamonte, Gulialmus de,
    647
  Portu, Çanachius de, 882
  Simitecollo, Michaletus,
    477
  Simon, 119
  Theologiti, Dimitrius, 119
  Vivianus, magister, 820
Çermana
  Agnes, 526
Cermia
  Lingiachus de, iudeus, 650
Certaçena
  Maria, ex-slave, 827
Cervia
  Francesquinus de, 937
Cesena
  Andreas de, frater, lector
    Fratrum Minorum,
    366, 371
Cethus
  Salamone, 121
Chaçaba
  casale, 841
Chafatena
  Marula, 946
Chagi
  iudeus, 200
Chalamona
  Petrus, episcopus, 13
Chaleucena
  Papadhia, 262

Chali, see Cali
chaligaria, see caligaria
Chalocheranna
  Chalamascho, tu, 838
  iudea, 127
Chamesi
  casale, 638
Chana
  iudea, 175
Chanal, see Canale
Chandachiteno
  Potha, 39
Chandachiti, Chandachyti
  Agnes, widow of
    Nicolaus, 824
  Andronicus, 824
  Andronicus, son of
    Georgius, 825
  Antonius, 305
  Cali, widow of Iohannes,
    296
  Erini, wife of Hemanuel,
    cillerarius, 840
  G., 575, 624
  Georgius, 240, 287, 825
  Georgius, sutor, 79
  Georgius, notarius, 840
  Hemanuel, cilerarius, 840
  Hemanuel, speçapetra,
    819
  Ianetus, 824
  Iohannes, 296
  Maria tu, 824
  Michael, arcerius, 305
  Nicolota, wife of
    Antonius, 305
  Nicolaus, 824, 946
Chandaquitena, 240
  Agnes, 9
Chandaquitus
  Georgius, 137
Chanea, 592, 614, 650, 669,
  809
  David, iudeus, 650, 954
  Ploreo, Michael, 79
  Potha de, 643
  Sanudo, Thomadho, 347
Chanioti

Cherana, 39
  Michael, 655
Charandina, see Carandina
Charandione
  Antonius, speciarius, 855
Charca
  casale, 25
Charchia
  Cali, daughter of
    Michael, 254
  Michael, 287
Charchiadena, 785
Charcomata
  Michael, 254
Charchiopulo
  Georgius, cerdo, 902
Charchopulo
  Nicolaus, 703
Chardamina
  Eudhochya, 672
Charia
  iudea, 200
Chaselerus, 568
Chastarena
  Luludhia, calogrea, 772
Chasturi
  Hemanuel, 309
Chasuri
  Herini, iudea, widow of
    Sambatheus, iudeus,
    809
  Sambatheus, iudeus, 809
Chatarucia, see Catarucia
Chatelano, see Catellano
Chavi
  Alexandria, de, iudeus,
    174
  iudeus, 174, 180
Chefala
  calogerus, 966, 980
  Germanus, monachus,
    784
  Germanus, papas, 912
  Grimano, papas,
    calogerus, 908
  papas, 894
Chefala S. Salvator
  papas, calogerus, 871

Chera
  Theodora, 706
Chera Chosti
  ecclesia, 257, 468, 569
  Macrimale de, papas, 19
Chera Ialini
  ecclesia Dei Genitricis,
    306
Chera Manolitissa
  ecclesia, 18, 223, 431
Chera Pissiotissa, 925
  Constantinus de, papas, 18
  ecclesia, 257, 614
  Nicolaus de, papas, 867
Cheraffa
  Iohannes, 788
  Maria, wife of Iohannes,
    788
Cherana, 15, 90, 146, 294,
  316, 452, 466, 491, 523,
  617, 634, 639, 730, 972
  Adrosi, servicialis,
    daughter of Marcus,
    826
  ancila, 191, 309
  Armachena, 948
  Asprogerena, 97
  baiula, 54, 149, 530, 576
  Belança, iudea, wife of
    Helia, iudeus, 200
  calogrea, 970
  calogrea, ex-slave, 984
  Carpathia, 303, 835
  Casanena, 680
  Chanioti, 39
  Corfioti, wife of Nicolaus,
    238
  Damiano, tu, 519
  ex-slave, 383
  famula, 811
  Focha, wife of Georgius,
    729
  Francho, wife of Marcus,
    barbitonsor, 574
  Feragudho, wife of
    Marcus, 601
  iudea, 459, 608, 639, 954
  iudea, called Pangalia,

  widow of Ioa, iudeus,
    200
  Maçamurdi, widow of
    Michael, 135
  Magerse, 571
  Malvasiota, 244
  Mauro, 588
  Melissina, 29
  Miçopulla, 804
  Moriutissa, 633
  nena, 473, 692, 826
  Paulopulo, ex-slave, 735
  Ploreo, daughter of
    Georgius, 466
  Prasino, widow of
    Michael, 146
  Promondini, 724
  Quirino, de ca', 140
  Quirino, wife of Leo,
    beccarius, 655
  Rossa, 786
  Sarasin, 656
  Scarpantho, de, 833
  Sclavo, widow of
    Iacobus, 523
  Selopulena, 326
  servicialis, 588
  Siligardena, 542
  sister of Sarasinus, 49
  slave, 223, 262, 288, 370,
    411, 530, 562, 568,
    569, 614, 620, 669,
    751
  Soleis, wife of Laurencius
    de, 794
  Vachere, daughter of Leo,
    523
  Venetando, 669
Cherannus
  Condoianopullo, 727
Cherarini
  Theologo, 713
Cherassia
  casale, 362, 778
  serventaria, 86
Cherchelli
  G., 828
  Nicolaus, papas, 98

Cherchi
  Symon, marescalcus, 738
Cherchioli
  Georgius, 384
  Iohannes, 384
  Maria, wife of Iohannes,
    384
Cherchelli
  Iohannes, 724
  Georgius, 350
  Marula, wife of Iohannes,
    724
Cheretena
  Aniça, 852
Cheriani, 640, 654
Cherianus
  papas, 802
Chersonisso
  Condocalo, Costas, de,
    287
Chiarana, see Cherana
Chiefala
  Georgius, 517
Chieli
  Psimeni, 545
Chierachi
  ex-slave, 568
Chierina
  mother of Vasilius, 39
Chiladini
  slave, 491
Chiliachus
  Pervolari, 911
Chiliopulo
  Iohannes, 622
Chilonissa
  Helena, 904
Chiloplenna
  Aniça, 622
Chimefti
  iudea, 631
China
  Vido, Nicolaus, 806
Chinamo
  locus, 525, 591
Chiparisu, 425
Chira Manolitissa, see Chera
  Manolitissa

Çorçina / Cornario

Çorçina, 442
Çorçinus, 976
Çorçius
   Smalino, de, 941
Çordanidena, 796
Çordanino
   Mariçoli, wife of
      Nicoletus, 490
   Nicoletus, 490
Çordan
   Vigonça, de, 826
Çordano
   Çaneta, wife of Iohannes,
      de Venetiis,
      coraçanus, 935
   Çordanus, son of Iohannes
      de, 935
   Hemanuel de, 764
   Iohannes de, de Venetiis,
      coraçanus, 935
Çordanus
   Çordano, son of Iohannes
      de, 935
Cordeferro, Cordefer
   Benevenuta, daughter of
      Rogerius, 26
   Çaneta, sister of Iohannes,
      25
   Caterina, wife of
      Rogerius, 24
   Fenga, wife of Iacobus, 24
   Iacobus, 24, 136, 521
   Iohannes, 25
   Maria, daughter of
      Matheus, 25
   Matheus, 25
   Mirabella, daughter of
      Rogerius, 25
   Rogerius, 24
Corento
   Michael de, slave, 242
coretum, 9
Corfe
   cavalleria, 334
Corfioti
   Cherana, wife of
      Nicolaus, 238
   Iohannes, 39

Nicolaus, 238
Corigiano
   Iacobus, 8
Corintho
   Andreas, 738
   Bartholomeus de, papas,
      monacus, 341
Cornario, Corner, 265, 671
   Agnes, daughter of
      Andreas, 250
   Agnes, daughter of
      Iohannes, 969
   Agnes, daughter of
      Nicolaus, 909
   Agnes, wife of Andreas,
      225
   Agnes, wife of
      Chornarachus, 541
   Albertinus, 204, 308
   Alexius, 330
   Alexius de domu maiori,
      206, 226, 314, 331,
      360
   Andreas, 26, 225, 250,
      257, 262, 266, 271,
      287, 331, 360, 364,
      746, 861, 871, 898,
      909, 956, 967, 993
   Andreas, de domu maiori,
      833, 912
   Andreas, de Venetiis, 265
   Andreas, son of Iacobus,
      57, 62
   Andreas, son of Marcus,
      de domu maiori, 314
   Aniça, 833, 835
   Aniça, wife of Georgius,
      arcerius, 585
   Antonius, murarius, 110
   Avanante, wife of
      Philipus, 962
   Ca', 542, 571, 992
   Cali, wife of Iohannes,
      788
   Chornarachus, 541
   Cicali, 370
   Constantinus, 508, 569
   Cornarola, daughter of

   Marcus, de domu
      maiori, 257
   Donatus, 531, 545
   Eudoquia, 776
   Eugenia, monacha, 192
   Filipo, 340
   Flordelisa, wife of
      Iohannes, called
      Sclavinus, 312
   Francisca, wife of
      Iacobus, 270
   Francesco, son of
      Iohanninus, 340
   Franciscus, 314, 332, 969
   Frangula, daughter of
      Andreas, 250
   Georgius, 533, 757
   Georgius, arcerius, 585
   Helena, 290, 849
   Helena, daughter of
      Andreas, 250
   Helena, wife of Iohannes,
      741
   Hemanuel, 707, 757
   Hurssa, 900
   Iacoba, wife of Alexius,
      de domu maiori, 332
   Iacobellus, 876
   Iacobina, 204, 257
   Iacobina, wife of Alexius,
      de domu maiori, 360
   Iacobina, wife of
      Andreas, 360
   Iacobus, 270, 290, 577,
      656
   Iacobus, called Maçaroni,
      257, 271
   Ieronimus, 708
   Iohannes, 75, 89, 108,
      157, 171, 206, 207,
      247, 262, 266, 308,
      312, 430, 560, 618,
      671, 741, 742, 788,
      819, 967-969
   Iohannes, de domu
      maiori, 62, 182, 252,
      314, 643, 834
   Iohannes, called

Lambardo, Marinus, 213
Liveri, Georgius, 213
Cortaci
    Andronicus, papas, 697
    Iohannes, 34
Corteler
    Missina, Nicolaus de, 559
Cortesano
    Hemanuel, 793
    Iohanachius, 607
Cortese
    Felix, 684
Cortesella
    Alexander de, 762
cortina, cortinum, 529, 637
Cosiropula, 181
Costa
    Petrus de la, notarius curie
        maioris, 355
Costancia, see Constancia
Costancius, see Constanciu
Costanda
    Languvardo, 616
Costantius, see Constancius
Costas, 548, 799
    Acardo, 792
    Barboso, 798
    Bono, 40
    Bonsignore, de, 715
    Brunello, villanus, 876
    Çambi, 98
    Chisamodi, son of Stratigi, 953
    Cladho, 894
    Condocalo, de Chersorusso, 287
    Condoiani, 107
    Condoleo, 994
    Condotodoro, 390
    Crasudhi, 77
    Davallerio, 708
    Epifani, 431
    famulialis, 315
    famulus, 964
    Filachanevo, peliparius, 113
    Franco, 133
    Gerardo, villanus, 447

Granella, servitor, 806
Gripioti, preco, 912
Gulambe, villanus, 799
Ialina, 696
Livano, servicialis, 904
Maçamano, villanus, 705
Marchyano, 238
Maurica, 933
Metupa, 970, 983
Mino, 74
Modhino, 770
Monomato, 386
Moscomili, 50
Musurachi, 216
papas, 796
Pefani, 40
Petronicola, 532
Pulladi, 710
Rosselo, 8
Russea, villanus, 302
Sagitta, son of Nicolaus, 119
seler, of Constantinople, 561
servo, slave, 370
Siribari, 679
slave, 122, 218, 363, 397, 420
Spiga, de, 899
Tarte, murarius, 770
Theofilo, 614
Thocharopulo, called Ripus, 845
Trivisano, son of Nicolaus, 129
Varucha, 506
villanus, 799
Vitalis, incantator, 577
Çostena, 627
Costicena
    Cornario, Maria, 110
Costinus
    Quirino, 746
Costomiri
    Helena, daughter of Stamatinus, 303
    Stamatinus, 303
Cota, 318, 574

Cotanto
    Georgius, called Mandrara, 946
    Maria, 375
Çote
    Catarucia, daughter of Nicoletus, de Venetiis, 409
    Nicoletus, de Venetiis, 409
Cothrologo
    Zana de, 351
Coti,
    Marcus, 705
    Sophia, wife of Marcus, 705
Çoti
    Verivo, 984
covercerum, 29, 548
coverçurum, 466
Çoya, 883
Craliça, 504
Crasudhena
    Maria, 77
Crasudhi
    Aniça, daughter of Vasili, 77
    Costas, 77
    Georgius, 77
    Hemanuel, 77
    Sophia, daughter of Vasili, 77
    Vasili, 77
Cremona
    Bertulinus de, frater, 556
    Bonacursius de, 55
    Caliça, daughter of Frangulus de, 814
    Casamal, Cominus de, 511
    Frangulus de, 814
    Margarita, wife of Nicolaus, 251
    Marinus de, preco, 497
    Nicolaus de, 251
    Rossetus da, 711
    Thomas de, 251
    Ysabella de, 764

Crenu
Herini, 298
Cricheli
Georgius, 281
Crescentio, Crisenço
Çorçi de, 888
Erchielda de, 888
Franguli de, 888
Georgius de, 973
Richioldi de, 974
Crisiona
casale, 315
Cristina
Aniça, monaca, nena, 54
ex-slave, 868
Mauroceno, widow of
Antonius, 762
Cristo
Michael de lo, papas, 514
Cruce
Franciscus de, notarius,
195
Crusafa, 411, 428
Crusi
Fuscari, 852
slave, 334
Crusollura, see Chrussolura
Crussiona
casale, 694
Crusso
Georgius, 933
Crussolura, see Chrussolura
crux, 324, 773, 959
crux sanctorum, 393
Çuba, 318
Cucamoni, 672
Cuchena
Thomasina, 931
Çuchiena
venderigola, 710
Cuchuro
Georgius, 785
Cucilli
Agnes, 776
Cucivena
Maria, 468
cucubina
Margarita, 546

Cuculino
Donçorçi, Nicolaus, 764
Cuculinus
Çorçi, de, 794
Çorçi, Marcus,
subdiaconus, 377
Cuçumanos
Maçamandi, Hemanuel,
224
Cuçupa
Moscana, nena, 827
Cuffopulina
Maria, 561
Cufoplectu
Catafigi, calogrea, 766
Çufredus
Lupino, 8
Mauroceno, ducha Crete,
660
Çulian
Agnesina, wife of
Antonius de, 989
Antonius de, 989
Culiana
Moscana, 250
Çulianenas
Cali, 636
Çuliano
Andriola, widow of
Leonardus, 418
Leonardus, 418
cultellum, 739
Cumaro
Samargias, iudeus, 821
Cumela
vinea, 202
Cumessareas
Potha, tis 94
cupa, cuppa, 755, 887
Georgius, 329
çupa, 375, 526
çupani
çuponum, 711, 959
Cuppum, 81, 96
Constancia, 4
Cura
Marula tu, 705
Curacia, 9

Curadena
Erini, 675
curadentum, 535, 640, 654
Curado
Georgius de, marangonus,
9
curator
Puladha, Marcus, 225
Cursari
Aniça, wife of Hemanuel,
822
Cali, daughter of
Hemanuel, 822
Eudochia, daughter of
Hemanuel, 822
Georgius, son of
Hemanuel, 822
Hemanuel, 822
Herini, daughter of
Hemanuel, 822
Iohannes, son of
Hemanuel, 822
Maria, daughter of
Hemanuel, 822
Curtachi
Hemanuel, 734
Cureni
Aniça, ancila, 233
Curi
Filipa, 689
Çuri
Geço, 107
curia Crete, 882
Curinoclissi
Iohannes, 860
Çurlopula
Potha, 281
Curtalo
Andreas, papas, 149
Bartholomeus, 1
Curte
Franciscus de, 155
Curtesi
Çanina, 972
Helea, wife of Salomon,
142
Salomon, iudeus, 142
Curtessena, 849

Curtesus
  iudeus, 608
Curtichi
  Hemanuel, 891
  Stephanus, papas, 39
curtina, 273
Çusamana
  Pascaligo, wife of
    Antonius, 423
cusinellum, cusinelus, 399,
  781, 868
cusita, 318
Custemona, 802
Çustignan
  Mariçoli, 931
Çusto
  Micael, clericus, 424, 434
custos
  Catellanos, Iohannes, 518
custos Fratrum Minorum
  Peyra, Antonius de, frater,
    352
custos S. Titi
  Helena, 814
Cutaioti
  Constancius, 281
  Constantinus, 589, 751
  Hergini, wife of Petrus,
    751
  Matheus, 471
  Paulus, 751, 956
  Petrus, 299, 751
Cutemi
  Soi, wife of Stephanus,
    168
  Stephanus, 168
Cutralli
  Iani, 366
Cutruli
  Calognomo, Georgius,
    called, 397
Cuvoclissio
  Iohannes, 855
  Iohannes, papas, 145
Cypro
  Dominicus de, 190, 272
Cyprus, 190, 208, 255, 264,
  281

Dacri
  Georgius, 728
Dadho, Dado
  Franciscus, 7, 78, 962
  Frangulius, 853, 858
  Herigina, daughter of
    Nicolaus, 878
  Iacoba, wife of Zaninus,
    857
  Iohannes, 9, 27, 254, 656
  M., 643
  Marcus, 653
  Maria, wife of Franciscus,
    9
  Nicolaus, 853, 878
  Rolandus, 776
  Stamatius, 134
  Zanina, daughter of
    Nicolaus, 853
  Zaninus, 853, 857
Dafnes, Dhafnes
  casale, 240, 778
Dalmario
  Nicolaus, presbyter, 272
Dalnpnena
  Nicoleta, 508
Damaruca, 93
Dambaniça
  magistra, 553
Damiano
  Agnes, 76
  Apostoli, sutor, 75
  Cali, wife of Michatius,
    690
  Cherana tu, 519
  Franciscus, 686
  Maria, wife of Apostoli,
    sutor, 76
  Michael, 76
  Michatius, sutor, 690
  Nicolaus, 690, 732, 977
Damianus, 519
  Clarencia, de, peliparius,
    672
Damiladena, 968
Dandula
  Dandulo, daughter of

Nicolaus Belinus,
  202, 634
Dandulo, Dandolo
  Agnes, 370, 716, 838,
    916
  Agnes, wife of Nicolaus
    Belinus, 201, 389
  Alexius, son of Nicolaus,
    972
  Andreas, 259, 415, 504,
    689, 959, 972
  Antonius, civis
    Veneciarum, 829
  Belinus, 505
  Caterina, daughter of
    Belinus, 505, 633
  Clara, 93
  Dandula, daughter of
    Nicolaus Belinus,
    202, 634
  Donatus, 201, 353, 508,
    635, 679, 689, 971,
    972
  Elena, widow of Marcus,
    679
  Elena, wife of Franciscus,
    985
  Francisca, wife of
    Belignus, 633
  Francischina, daughter of
    Iohannes, 390
  Franciscus, 985
  Franciscus, son of
    Nicolaus, 972
  G., 834
  Georgius, 836, 954, 970,
    975
  Gibertus, consiliarius,
    401
  Gilbertus, ducha Crete,
    123
  Gratonus, de Venetiis,
    958
  Helena, 716
  Helena, daughter of
    Donatus, 635
  Hemanuel, 88
  Hemanuel, clericus, 544

Henricus, 207, 959
Henricus, son of Thomas,
411
Hergina, 705, 972, 985
Herigina, 909
Iacobus, 705
Iohannes, 201, 389, 433,
679, 688, 836, 972
Iohannes, clericus, 584
Iohannes, ex-aurifex, 853
Iohannes, frater, 351
Iohannes, miles, 959
Leo, 64, 795
Lio, 390
Madalucia, 829
Magdalucia, wife of
Gratonus, de Venetiis,
959
Marchesina, 689
Marco, 336, 689
Marcus, 88, 201, 207,
296, 366, 508, 635,
679, 688, 834, 959,
971
Margarita, 799, 834
Maria, 465
Marula, daughter of
Nicolaus, 972
Nicolaus, 16, 504, 679,
689, 829, 971
Nicolaus Belinus, 201,
258
Nicoleta, wife of
Nicoletus, 353, 354
Nicoleto, 689
Nicolota, daughter of
Marcus, 296
Ninda, soror, 23, 93, 504
Pantalea, wife of Andreas,
259, 415
Petrus, 470, 522, 959
Petrus, presbyter,
capellanus ecclesie
Crete, 428
Petrus, presbyter, notarius,
195, 205, 412
Philipa, wife of Nicolaus,
971

Potha, widow of
Hemanuel, 88
Thomado, 390
Thomas, 202
Thomas, son of Gratonus,
de Venetiis, 960
Thomasina, 23, 365
Thomasina, wife of
Iohannes, 389
Uclinus, 256
Vidal, 390
Vitalis, 202
Zanachius, 353, 365
Danese
Cali, 113
Dani
Moço, 657
Daniel, 585
Chapella, 951
Favaço, speciarius, 785
Gastrea, ieromonachus,
208
Greco, 283
Portono, da, 711
Quirino, 84, 269
Danipella
Costancius, frater, 813
Dardi
Contarini, 896
Venerio, 339
Dardius
Balbi, 246
Daria
Corario, daughter of
Maria, 81
Quirino, wife of Andreas,
333
Quirino, wife of Paulus,
460
Dario
Iohannes, 88, 108, 226
Dato
Adhamus, 26
Theodora, wife of
Adhamus, 26
Davallerio
Costas, 708
Georgius, 708

Stamatinus, 708
Davançago
Dominicus, 402
David, Davit
Casani, iudeus, 944, 988
Chanea, de, iudeus, 650,
954
iudeus, 246, 716
decanus, 421
decanus Cretensis
Riçardi, Antonius, 412
Decretale cum apparatu
Bernardi, 412
Dei Genitrix
casale, Polemissa, 268
scola, 281
Dei Genitrix, Adhigitria
ecclesia, 775
Dei Genitrix Angelorum
ecclesia, 275
Dei Genitrix Chera Chosti
ecclesia, 281, 282
Dei Genitrix Chera Ialini
ecclesia, 223, 228, 231
Dei Genitrix Chera Pissiotissa
ecclesia, 266
Dei Genitrix Dhiavatini
ecclesia, 236
monasterium, 236
Dei Genitrix Domina
Angelorum
ecclesia, 240
Dei Genitrix Manolitissa
ecclesia, 182
Dei Genitrix Militum
ecclesia, 249, 256, 262
Dei Genitrix Morfitanissa
ecclesia, 242
Dei Genitrix Muctari
ecclesia, 271
Dei Genitrix Odhigitria
ecclesia, 278
Dei Genitrix Panagia
ecclesia, 240, 278
Dei Genitrix Panimnito
ecclesia, 240
Dei Genitrix Perimblepto
ecclesia, 769

Dei Genitrix S. Maria, Marçala
  ecclesia, 785
Dei Genitrix Theoschepasto
  ecclesia, 278
Delenda
  Iacobus de, 789
Delphinus, Delfinus
  Vedoaciis, de, 841, 842,
    846, 850
Delphyno
  Bernardus, 853
  Nicolaus, consiliarius, 365
Dema
  Ravichus, castellanus, 120
Demitrius, see Dimitrius
Deo
  Iohannes de, clericus, 369
Deolaço
  Petrus, 273
Descamato
  Marchesina, 840
Desde
  Gerardus, 926
  Iohannes, 259
  N., 487
  Nicolaus, 491
  Nicolinus, 21, 31
  Petrus, frater, 519
Deso, Desso
  Angelus, diaconus, 406
  Chali, widow of Marcus,
    406
  Filipus, preco, 403
  Marcus, 406
  Petrus, 553
Despelo
  Iohannes, 574
Despotato
  Maria, wife of Michael,
    205
  Michael de, 205
Dharchana, 73
Dhermata
  locus, 247
Dhimitreli
  monasterium, S. Georgius,
    310
Dhramitino

Marcus, villanus, 931
Dhrimocatissa
  territorium, 792
Dhuli, 26
Diaco
  Iohannes, 287
diacona
  S. Georgius, calogrea,
    116
diaconissa
  Herini, calogrea, 351
diaconus
  Albiço, Antonius, 421
  Deso, Angelus, 406
  Fuschi, Nicoletus, 663
  Georgius, 303
  Gisi, Remundinus, 411
  Mudacio, Iohannes, 442
  Mutio, Marcus, 429
  Venetiarum, Nicolaus,
    420
  Vere, Marcus, 483
diaconus grecus
  Poliocto, Nicolaus, 849
Diamante, 23
Diana, 702
Diassidi, 649
Diesilo
  Marinus, 12
Diesolo, Diesulo
  Andriola, widow of
    Marinus, 648
  Iacobus, 12
  Marinus, 648
Diesulo Rosso
  Leo, auxilator, 773
Diminiti, Diminitis
  Aniça, daughter of
    Georgius, 802
  Cali, widow of Lucas,
    311
  Georgius, 802
  Lucas, 304, 311, 601
  Theodorus, 123
Diminuero
  Aderius, 373, 374, 376-
    378, 380-382, 384,
    385, 387-389, 391,

393, 394, 400
Dimistichina, 552
Dimitra, 10, 710
Dimitri, 931
  bulgarus, slave, 370
  Marci, 390
  Milano, de, 90
  slave, 311
Dimitria, 519
Dimitrius, Demitrius, 943
  Alexandro, 782
  Alexiopulo, 940
  Amarando, 854
  Beto, 975
  Blachernitissa, de, papas,
    212
  Caco, 918
  Catellan, 131
  Conapioti, 789
  Contareno, 384
  Donçorçi, son of
    Nicolaus, 764
  Draganno, 850
  Felchelcha, son of Conço
    de, 945
  Fuscolo de Chorono, 803
  Grimaldo, 223
  Manchaffa, 846
  Marçangelo, 218, 641
  Marcatante, 946
  Massaro, 894
  Mudacio, scutiferus, 294
  Nuto, 860
  Paneromitti, 388
  Papas, 542
  Pasqualigo de
    Nigroponte, 773
  Penerimiti de Musco, 303
  presbyter, 455
  Quirino, papas, 877
  Roddo, de, 854
  Sclavo, 736
  Siropulo, 883, 965
  slave, 31, 472, 491
  Stratigopulo, 280
  Thalasino, 589, 604
  Theologiti, cerdo, 119
Dimitropulo

Doncena, 540
Donçorçi
    Agnes, 683
    Candelorus, son of
        Nicolaus, 764
    Dominicus, son of
        Nicolaus, 764
    Marcus, presbyter, 866
    Monforte, wife of
        Nicolaus, called
        Cuculino, 764
    Nicolaus, called Cuculino,
        764
Dondade
    Erizo, 733
Dondi
    Donatus, 663, 664
    Iacobina, wife of
        Iohannes, 344
    Iohannes, 34, 36, 211,
        228, 344, 383
    Iohannes, peliparius, 264
    L., 388
    Leonardus, 771
    Nicolaus, 211, 228, 535
    Paschalinus, 553, 556
    Pasqualis, 559
Dondo
    Marinus, 137
Done
    Antonius de le, peliparius,
        137
    Heloise, daughter of
        Antonius de le,
        peliparius, 137
    Herini, wife of Antonius
        de le, peliparius, 137
    Iohannes, son of Antonius
        de le, peliparius, 137
    Margarita, daughter of
        Antonius de le,
        peliparius, 137
Donne
    Petrus de le, presbyter,
        293, 574
Dono, Donno
    Bartholomeus, de Sithea,
        902

Cali, 802
Çanachi, 796
Constantia, widow of
    Nicolaus, 425
Cornarola, 776
Cornarola, widow of
    Iohannes, 250, 425
Francisca, 551
Francisca, widow of
    Paulus, 587
Franciscus, 637
Georgius, notarius
    Venetiarum, 973
Iacobina, wife of Petrus,
    637
Iacobus, 752, 889
Iohannes, 55, 59, 250,
    337, 346, 350, 355,
    362, 587, 643, 709,
    981
L., 649
Laurencius, 647, 651,
    652, 656, 673
Leonardus, 658
Marchesina, daughter of
    Nicolaus, de Sythia,
    637
Nicolaus, 425, 551
Nicolotus, 643
Octavianus, 24, 300
P., frater, 94
Pauletus, natural son of
    Petrus, 638
Paulus, 587, 637
Peracius, 337
Petrus, 24, 300, 587, 637,
    900
Ra., clericus, 569
Regina, 492
Yonigha, widow of
    Petrus, 587
Doria, 903
dota, 671
Doto
    Andreas, frater, 454
    Caloçesa, 317
    Georgius, son of Xenus,
        ex-slave, 581

    Iohannes, son of Xenus,
        ex-slave, 581
    Maria, wife of Xenus, ex-
        slave, 581
    Matheus, 581
    Michael, son of Xenus,
        ex-slave, 581
    Tomas, 449
    Xenus, ex-slave, 581
Douca
    Petrus de la, 268
Draco
    Gabriel, 538
    Maria, daughter of
        Gabriel, 538
Draga
    Venerio, wife of
        Bartholomeus, preco
        curie Crete, 463
Draganno
    Dimitrius, 850
Dragomano
    Iohannes, 967
    Marcus, 968
Dragonese
    Iohannes, 557
    Margarita, widow of
        Iohannes, 557
Dragonus
    Geno, 387
Drapera, Draprera
    Hergina, 851
    Nicolinus, 851
dreçati, 541, 547, 576
dreçatori, 49, 81, 271, 438,
    629, 707, 862, 959
drecera, 560
driçolis, 314
Drossio
    Iohannes, 682
Drossu, 788
ducha Crete
    Baduario, Albanus, 831
    Baduario, Petrus, 205,
        291, 309, 639
    Bono, Dominicus, 953
    Cornario, Marcus, 56, 78,
        296, 610, 651-653,

655-659, 662
Cornario, Petrus, 365
Dandulo, Gilbertus, 123
Geno, Andreas, 975
Geno, Marcus, 915, 993
Gradonico, Iohannes, 512,
746, 748, 752
Gradonico, Marcus, 266
Grimani, Marinus, 198,
300
Iustiniano, Iustinianus,
462
Mauro, Donatus, 760,
762, 952
Mauroceno, Çufredus,
660
Mauroceno, Iohannes, 472
Mauroceno, Marinus, 237,
333, 362, 725
Mozenigo, Petrus, 401
Dulcena, 897
Dulcis
Petrus, 224
Duodo
Andreas, son of Petrus, de
Venetiis, 847
Iohannes, 848
Iohannes, de Venetiis, 399
Petrus, de Venetiis, 847
Victor, 847
duplerium, 366
Duracio
Andreas de, 859
Zaninus, son of Andreas
de, 859
Durente
Marula, 854
Philipus, 855
Dusano
Raphael, 486

Ecclesia
Aius Pandes, 846, 849
Archadiensis, 859
Archistratigi, 757
Beata Maria Virgo, 799
Beatus Antonius, 742, 746

Beatus Franciscus, 23
Beatus Iacobus de
Gallicia, 379
Chera Chosti, Chiera
Chosti, 257, 468, 569
Chera Manolitissa, 18,
223, 431
Chera Pissiotissa, 257,
266, 614
Christo, 468
Christo de la Vicuta, 574
Christo Suriano, 766
Christo lo Chiefala, 508
Dei Genitrix, Odhigitria,
775
Dei Genitrix Angelorum,
275
Dei Genitrix Chera
Chosti, 281, 282
Dei Genitrix Chera Ialini,
228, 231
Dei Genitrix Dhiavatini,
236
Dei Genitrix Domina
Angelorum, 240
Dei Genitrix, casale
Polemissa, 268
Dei Genitrix Manolitissa,
182
Dei Genitrix Militum,
249, 256, 262
Dei Genitrix
Morfitianissa, 242
Dei Genitrix Muctari, 271
Dei Genitrix Odhigitria,
278
Dei Genitrix Panagia,
240, 278
Dei Genitrix Panimnito,
240
Dei Genitrix,
Perimblepto, 769
Dei Genitrix S. Maria,
Marçala, 785
Dei Genitrix
Theoschepasto, 278
Dominus Deus et Salvator
Noster Yhesus

Christus, 240, 284
Faneromeni, 755
Fratres Heremite, 37, 44,
53, 57, 158, 162,
182, 355, 417
Fratres Minores, 11, 182,
370, 417, 567, 611
Fratres Predicatores, 92,
95, 103, 266, 431,
432, 455, 600
Maria Magdalena, 179
Mt Sinai, 466, 538, 539
Neamoni, 802, 832
Odigitria, 753, 769
Panimnito, 475, 771
Pisiotissa, 542
SS Apostoli, 47, 281, 303
SS Apostoli, Marula, 775
SS Apostoli, Pigaidulia,
228
SS Petrus et Paulus, 863
S. Agnes, de Venetiis, 71
S. Andreas, 303
S. Andreas monacarum,
856
S. Anna, 8, 101, 306,
222, 308, 466, 468,
603, 730, 795, 911
S. Anna, Chanea, 30
S. Anna, Fundico, 18
S. Anna, Veni, 607
S. Annastassia, 730
S. Antonius, 20, 154,
266, 327, 417, 425,
461, 687, 689, 700,
705, 711, 868, 871,
873, 875, 882, 893,
959, 964, 966, 968,
971, 976
S. Antonius, Belvidere,
30
S. Antonius Grecorum,
871
S. Athanasius, 671, 966,
968
S. Barbara, 76, 103, 182,
324, 327, 431, 461,
557, 560, 816

S. Barnaba, Marçala, 784

S. Çacharia de Venetiis, 70

S. Caterina, 19, 20, 83, 90, 96, 103, 106, 107, 337, 417, 434, 473, 482, 552, 654, 806

S. Caterina monacarum, 856

S. Chyrilus Sochorum, 222

S. Clara, 899

S. Crux, Caçamba, 278

S. Dei Genitrix, Chera Chosti, 980

S. Dei Genitrix, Odigitria, 173

S. Dimitrius, 6, 10, 101, 118, 119, 229, 775

S. Dominica, 228

S. Dominicus, 17, 452

S. Donatus, Chelia, 679

S. Franciscus, 25, 35, 44, 57, 69, 78, 80, 109, 158, 185, 189, 233, 241, 242, 252, 284, 292, 294, 327, 347, 360, 370, 409, 417, 419, 463, 582, 637, 656, 675, 682, 687, 689, 714, 778, 782, 806, 857, 859, 905, 974, 982

S. Georgius, 20, 30, 81, 327, 402, 417, 420, 433, 582, 838, 878

S. Georgius, Argiropigadhi, 595

S. Georgius, Belvidere, 538

S. Georgius, Catocastri, 542

S. Georgius, Cavura, 281, 641, 992

S. Georgius, Dhiasotti, 788

S. Georgius, Dhotano, 122

S. Georgius, Gasunoti,

542

S. Georgius Georgii Camarioti, 542

S. Georgius monacarum, 473

S. Georgius monacarum Fardulari, 856

S. Georgius, Muglino, 770

S. Georgius, Perati, 769

S. Georgius, Pendamodhi, 538

S. Georgius Penetadhi, 107

S. Georgius, Puncta, Ponta, 37, 58, 73, 81, 103, 187, 425, 434, 461, 647, 782, 853

S. Georgius, Staurachi, 288

S. Georgius, Steriano, 172

S. Georgius, Tamura, 774

S. Georgius Venerio, 103

S. Georgius, Veneto Venetus, 324, 327, 682

S. Georgius Vido, 266

S. Georgius, Votirioti, 30

S. Helia, 802

S. Iacobus, 61, 96, 154, 461, 530, 714, 885, 924, 928, 930, 976

S. Iohannes, 964, 968

S. Iohannes Baptista, 239

S. Iohannes Baptista burgi Sithie, 990

S. Iohannes Crisostomo, 588

S. Iohannes Crisostomo, Meta, 18

S. Iohannes, Marula, 940, 980

S. Iohannes, Pre Iacumicio, 749

S. Iohannes Evangelista, castrum burgi, 792

S. Iohannes Liberator,

859

S. Iohannes, Palmosa, Polmosa, 30, 792

S. Iohannes Theologa, Dermata, 695

S. Iohannes Theologi, 351, 753

S. Iohannes verberatorum, 838

S. Iulianus, 69

S. Laçaro, 18, 30, 141, 461, 478, 796

S. Liberalis, 514

S. Liberalis, Mitilini, 18

S. Lucia, 597, 793

S. Marcus, 3, 158, 463, 683, 714, 939

S. Maria, 222, 320, 607, 887

S. Maria, Angelis, 411

S. Maria Angelorum, 20, 148

S. Maria Anunciatio, 793

S. Maria Baraterii, 222

S. Maria, burgo castri Belvedere, 402

S. Maria Calesiani, 329

S. Maria called Paliotissa, 878

S. Maria called Vigli, 904

S. Maria, Candelor, de la, 634

S. Maria castri Themensis, 617

S. Maria Chera Ialini, 306, 597

S. Maria Chera Chosti, 870

S. Maria, Coleliani, 595

S. Maria, Conave, 488

S. Maria Cruciferorum, 9, 20, 103, 117, 154, 162, 172, 182, 189, 190, 198, 225, 249, 266, 267, 270, 273, 324, 327, 337, 434, 436, 437, 439, 452, 461, 465, 469, 473,

Fertya
  Signolo, 776
festivitas Salvatoris, 982
feudum
  Larcana, 721
  Vutafu, 905
Feussini
  iudea, 127
Fidorus, 517
figura
  Virgin Mary, 96
Filachanevo
  Costas, peliparius, 113
  Georgius, 113
  Marcus, de Venetiis, 756
Filadelfino
  Constantinus, papas, 207
Filaretis
  Antonius de, 62
  Georgius de, 350
  Georgius de, notarius, 61,
    641
  Hergina, wife of Georgius
    de, 62
  Hergina, wife of
    Nicoletus, 641
  Iohaninus de, 62
  Nicoletus, 641
  Petrus de, 62
  Petrus de, frater, 350
Filareto
  Iohannes, 919
  Michael de, papas, 468
  Nicolaus, 59, 321, 322,
    327, 571, 869
Filathropino
  Nicolaus, papas, 877
Filarti, 542
Filarto
  Nicolaus, 312, 726
Fillartus
  Polliti, 517
Filielo
  Maria, 173
Filipa, see Philipa
Filipo, see Philipus
Filipus, see Philipus
Filippi

Antonius, 488
Filomatena
  Cali, 768
Fimi, 463
Fina
  Laurençio, de, 917
Fineta
  iudea, 127
Finichia
  casale, 989
Finsiadhura, 81
Fino
  Catarucia, 762
Firgavesto
  Andreas, 609
Firigo
  Nicolaus, 80
Firiolo
  Benedictus, 186
  Cecilia, wife of
    Leonardus, 480
  Iacobellus, son of
    Leonardus, 480
  Leonardus, 480
  Nicolaus, 25
  Nicolinus, 480
Firmo
  Andreas de, cancellarius
    Crete, notarius, 53,
    60, 68, 69, 198, 272,
    610, 644, 651-653,
    655-660, 662
  Antonius de, 38, 60, 78
  Çanachi de, noder, 783
  Caterina, daughter of
    Franciscus de,
    notarius, 67
  Franciscus de, notarius,
    43, 45, 60, 67, 165
  Georgius de, 198, 313
  Helena de, 198
  Iacobina, daughter of
    Franciscus de,
    notarius, 46
  Iacobus de, 602, 767, 768,
    770, 772, 773, 777,
    778
  Iacobus de, presbyter,

capellanus S. Tito,
    54, 193, 246, 568
  Iohannes de, 60, 67, 211,
    385
  Iohannes de, notarius,
    207, 925
  Marchesina, wife of
    Nicolaus de,
    notarius, 505
  Marcus de, murarius, 78
  Maria de, 78, 785
  Michael de, 211
  Nicolaus de, notarius,
    492, 505
  Paulus de, frater,
    guardianus conventus
    Minorum, 351
  Petrus de, 125, 339, 346
  Petrus de, notarius, 776
  Petrutius de, 711
  Rainaldus de, 809
  Rainaldus de, clericus,
    815
Fisicus, see Physicus
Fiugenichi
  serventaria, 125
Flabani
  Herini, 802
  Marinus, 78
Flabia
  Gratia, widow of Iacobus,
    cerdo, 91
  Iacobus, cerdo, 91
Flegotomo
  Andreas, 792
Flegotomopulo
  Maria, 145
flocum perlarum, 755
Flor
  Grimani, wife of
    Dominicus,
    cancellarius Crete,
    961
Flora, 568
  Nustri, 52
  Onufri, 565
  Rapani, widow of
    Iacobus, 572

Floramonte
  Mariçoli, 258
Floravans
  presbyter, 25
  Capellanus, presbyter, 548
Florencia, Florentia, 487
  Bernardus de, 907
  Carulus de, 130
  Gradonico, wife of
    Gabriel, 461
  Helena, wife of Lappus
    de, provisionatus, 737
  Ianora, wife of Petrus de,
    stipendiarius, 764
  Iohannes de, caporalis
    equester, 130
  Lappus de, provisionatus,
    737
  Petrus de, stipendiarius,
    764
  Scarsellis, Iohannes de,
    caporale, 738
  Tengo de, 287
Flordelisa
  Magno, wife of Marinus,
    976
Florera, 814
Floreta
  Selopulo, wife of
    Georgius, aurifex,
    792
Florevante
  Antonius, 932
  Francisca, 916
Flori
  Habramo, natural daughter
    of Petrus, 183
Fluru
  daughter of Bona, 37
Foca, Focha
  Cherana, wife of
    Georgius, 729
  Georgius, 729
  Hemanuel, 119
Fochianus
  papas, 984
Fodele
  Hemanuel, 660

Fodhelina
  Maria, 318
Fodhelo
  Iacobina, wife of
    Nicolaus, arcerius, 4
  Nicolaus, arcerius, 4
Fodhile
  Hemanuel, 53
Folchino
  Iacobus de, 166
Folisso
  Cali, widow of
    Laurencius, 534
  Laurencius, 534
Fontana
  Canale, widow of
    Antonius de, 810
  Fradello, wife of Thomas,
    286
  Micaletus de la, 399
Fontanella
  Aniça, 18
  Areti, 192
  Iohannes, 331
  Nicolaus, 156
Fonte
  Franciscus, 121
Forciano
  Cali, 242
Forcianudena
  Cali, 374
Fordelia, 530
  Fordelisa, Fordelixa, 835
  Sclença, 930
Forena
  Sophia, 801
Forlivio
  Morellus de, comestabilis
    pedester, 742
Formano
  Marcus, 440
Formarici
  Marula, daughter of
    Stephanus, 439
  Stephanus, 439
fornarius, furnarius
  Cofina, Leo, 33
  Suriano, Hemanuel, 698

Fornero
  Herini, 93
Fornita, 130
fornus, 698, 708
Fosalta
  Altinerius de, 398
  Civeçel de, comestabilis
    equester, civis
    tarvisanus, 398
  Conicia, wife of Civeçel
    de, 398
  Constancia, daughter of
    Civeçel de, 399
  Iohannes de, 398
  Toberto de, 399
Foscareno
  Blunda, wife of Claretus,
    264
  Cataruça, daughter of
    Marinus, called
    Slavus, 264
  Claretus, 264
  Dominicus, 264
  Marinus, called Slavus,
    264
  Nicolaus, 484
  Nicoletus, 474
  Paulus, 265, 374
  Sclavus, 265
Foscari
  Calica, natural daughter
    of Marchesinus, 296
  Francisca, wife of
    Sclavus, 415
  Marchesinus, 296
  Pothiti, widow of
    Marchesinus, 296
Foscareno, Foscarino,
  Fuscarino
  Çaninus, 974
  Franciscus, 937
  Iohannes, 887
  Nicolaus, 887
  Philipa, wife of
    Franciscus, 937
Foscolo, Fosculo, Fuscolo
  Andreas, presbyter, 469
  Blança, daughter of

761
Cervia, de, 937
Gisi, 690
Manolesso, son of
  Çaninus, 880
Mauro, 836
Medio, de, 905
Ragusio, son of Iohannes
  de, 909
Francisci
  Bartholomeus, notarius,
    179
Francisco
  Hemanuel de, 940
  Paulus de, 745
Franciscus, 394, 424, 431,
  699, 811, 868
  Abbate, de, 705
  Alemanis, de, magister,
    cirurgicus, 359
  Alexandrinus, 8
  aurifex, 933
  Balbi, 869
  Basino, de, 668
  Beatus, ecclesia, 23
  Belli, 169
  Bergamo, de, 130
  Bigoço, clericus, 441
  Bigolino, clericus, 413,
    424, 426
  Blanco, 800
  Bolan de Venetiis, 843
  Brixiano, peliparius, son
    of Bartholomeus, 437
  Çacharia, 162, 196, 288
  Çaconia, de, called
    Georgius, slave, 274
  Calcagno, de, comestabilis
    equester, 742
  Çampani, 294, 488
  Çane, 255
  Çapani, 159
  Caravella, 249, 267
  Caravello, 332, 369
  Castelle, da le,
    comestabilis, 511
  Catellano, 481
  Caucina, 497

Caucho, 570
Cauco, 957, 963
Çipro, de, 428
Colona, 5
Contareno, 249, 529, 531
Contareno de Venetiis,
  567
Cornario, 314, 332, 969
Cruce, de, notarius, 195
Curte, de, 155
Dadho, 7, 78, 962
Damiano, 686
Dandulo, 985
Dandulo, son of Nicolaus,
  972
discipulus, 561
Dono, 637
Faletro, clericus, 93
Firmo, de, notarius, 43,
  45, 60, 67, 165
Fonte, 121
Foscareno, 937
Foscolo, 203, 985
frater, 99, 432, 452
Garyo, de, 130
Geço, notarius, 337
Geno, 983
Gisi, son of Marinus, 759
Goço, notarius, 27
Gradonico, 172, 185
Grasso, presbyter, 890,
  894
Greco, 856
Grego, 942
Grimani, 177, 666
Grimaudo, de, 17
Iordanino, 7
Magister, de Venetiis, 805
Marca, de, frater, 57
Marci, 60, 273, 414, 577,
  902
Marino, 771
Mauroceno de Venetiis,
  355
Medio, de, 289, 723, 914,
  977
Mengolino, de, de Pirano
  de contrata S. Lucie,

831
Mesana, de, 816
Milano, de, 2, 4, 82, 90,
  152, 278, 282, 326
Mitra, de, 387
Molino, de, 24, 157, 260,
  285, 395, 396, 760
Molino, son of Leonardus
  de, 260
Montello, de, 936
Mudacio, 3, 223, 252,
  342
Pantaleo, 851
Paradiso, 812
Patras, de, 845
Pelegrino, 965
Pigoço, 821
Pisani, 649, 914
Pissano, 518
Placencia, de, 170, 250,
  403, 418
Pollis, de, 719
presbyter, 701
Ragusia, de, 257
Ramella, 69
Ranerio, de, 635
Raynerio, de, 505
Rimano, de, 44, 59, 85
Rimano, son of Balducius
  de, 85
Rogerio, de, 985
Samaco, frater, 57
Sanuto, 121
Sclavo, 188
Secreto, 777, 779
Senis, de, cirurgicus,
  magister, 203
Silvestro, 164
Suriano, 212
Tervisio, de, 78
Traversario, 849
Trivixio, de, famulus, 398
Valla, 924
Venerio, 225
Venetiano, 902
Vicencia, de, 724
Vigla, de, 377
Vigoncia, de, 290

Viligorde, de, 6
Visentino, 76
Zeniese, presbyter, 901
Zeniex, presbyter, 877
Zobles, de, 509
Franco
Bartholomeus, 5
Cecilia de, 375
Cherana, wife of Marcus,
barbitonsor, 574
Costas, 133
Georgius, son of
Theodorus, 133
Iohannes, frater, 35, 194,
249, 637
Iohaninus, 132
Marcus, 5
Marcus, barbitonsor, 573
Marcus, murarius, 6
Maria, wife of Marcus, 6
Maria, wife of Theodorus,
132
Moscana, widow of
Nicolaus, 574
Nicolaus, 574, 624
Paulus, 624
pelegrinus, 438
Theodorus, 132
Franculus
Cauco Clida, 943
Francunlius
Maçamano, 127
Francus, Franchus, 273,
343, 720
Baroci, 683
Begulinus, 416
Brixia, de, soldatus, 400
Geno, 795
Gradonico, 94
Gritola, 897
Paulopulo, 981
Placentia, de, 410
Placezia, de, 989
Rippa, de, 194
Rugerio, de, 743
Valla, 247
Visintino, 718
Frangia, Franghia

Balastro, 932
Sclença, 924
Venerio, 924
Frangius
Quirino, 838
Frangoleo, 474
Frangula, 125, 210, 223, 530,
776
Calergi, 243
Contareno, 260
Cornario, daughter of
Andreas, 250
Freganeschi, widow of
Donatus de, 54
Gisi, wife of Iohannes,
223
Gissi, 397
Gradonico, wife of
Nicolaus, 262
Habramo, wife of
Nicolaus, 302
Leçaca, 965
Molino, widow of
Hemanuel de, 250
Piamonte, wife of
Antonius de, 711
Quirino, 307
Sclavo, wife of Antonius,
656
Tonello, wife of Stamati,
766
Xidha, widow of
Leo, 665
Franguli
calogrea, 928
Crisenço, de, 888
Petta, 812
Frangulius
Caravello, 968
Coco, 371
Dadho, 853, 858
Mudacio, 914, 973
Mulino, de, 745
Venerio, 225
Vigoncia, de, 210, 919
Frangulla
Caravello, wife of
Franciscus, 369

Catellano, 330
Colona, daughter of
Iohannes, 891
Colona, piçocara,
daughter of Iohannes,
869
Manolesso, wife of
Çaninus, 880
soror, 342
Frangullus
caligarius, 787
Catellano, 604, 666
Cremona, de, 814
Gradonico, 242
Greco, 806
Porta, de, 554
Venerio, 422
Frangus, 514
Frani
Vlasto, 508
Frati Predicadori, see Fratres
Predicatores
Frari del Salvador, 989
Frari di San Piero, 677
Frari Remitani, see Fratres
Heremite
frasatura, 547
Frasenda, Frascenda, 473
Gradonico, wife of
Marcus, 209
Fratalia
S. Maria Grecorum, 655
frater
Abbate, Gabriel de,
provincialis Fratrum
Heremitarum, 990
Angelinus, episcopus
Sude, 273
Antonius, 302
Antonius, guardianus
Fratrum Minorum,
187
Baratius, 432
Baxilio, Dinande, 184
Bergamensis, Henricus,
80
Bergamo, Petrus de, 366
Bertucius, 37, 423

Andreas, called
  Maurogonato, 854
Andreas, ducha Crete, 975
Aniça, 854
Barbara, called
  Pascalicena, 924
Bonafans, wife of
  Matheus, 20, 547
Çanachius, 795
cha', 976
Dominicus, 204, 308
Dragonus, 387
Filipa, 920
Franciscus, 983
Francus, 795
G., 730
Georgius, 700, 737, 739,
  743, 747, 795, 867,
  870, 875
Helena, widow of
  Nicoletus, 646
Helena, wife of
  Dominicus, 204, 308
Hemanuel, 132
Herigena, wife of
  Marinus, 903
Herini, 93
Ianinus, 622
Iohannes, 258, 287, 795,
  880
Iohannes, Maurogonato,
  251
Iohannes, de Venetiis, 69
Iohanninus, de Venetiis,
  387
L., 644
Laurencius, 387, 509, 640
Leonardus, 657
Marcus, 144, 258, 482,
  619, 795
    Marcus, ducha Crete,
    915, 993
Margarita, soror, 920
Marinus, 903
Marula, soror, 982
Matheus, 20, 547
Nicolaus, 147, 224, 251,
  387, 629

Nicoletus, 903
Nicoletus, barbitonsor,
  646
Nicolota, wife of Marcus,
  619
Petrus, 680, 774, 969
Petrus, de Venetiis, 387
Ranucius, 387
Ranucius, de Venetiis,
  774
Regina, 30
Sclavus, 473
T., 373
Thodorellus, 374
Thomas, 877
Thomasina, 21
Georgia, 37, 95
  slave, 2
Georginus
  Milano, de, 4
Georgio, 362
  Dominicus, 779
  Dominicus, presbyter,
    352, 953
  Gracianus, 760
  Marcus, 820
  Mariçoli, widow of
    Marcus, 820
  Meliorinus, 245
  Nicoletus, notarius, 364
  Sancti, presbyter, 676
  slave, 218
Georgis
  Camulo, preco, 948
Georgius, 321, 395, 415, 662,
  692, 706, 808, 984
  Abbate, de, 219, 279,
    384, 803, 920
  Abramo, 689
  Achulo, slave, 224
  Aligaça, 73
  Aplada, 695
  Arbe, de, 976
  Arcoleo, villanus, 957
  Armino, cerdo, 552
  Avancio, de, 507
  Avini, 435
  Avonale, 987

Avonale, discipulus, 583
Avradho, 277
Aymo, 857
Aymo, notarius, 969
Barbafella, 428
Barbafella, aurifex, 240,
  643
Barbo, 351, 645, 665
Baxilio, 935
Belono, 315, 318
Beto, 975
Bolani, 867, 883
Boni, 881
Bono, 711
bordonarius, slave, 447
bulgarus, slave, 968
buticlarius, 233
Caco, 918, 923
Caco, son of Dimitrius,
  918
Çaconia, Franciscus de,
  slave, called, 274
Cafato, 221
Calergi, 189, 204, 337,
  614
Calognomo, called
  Cutruli, 397
Calopti, papas, 603
Canale, de, 241, 286
Çanpari, faber, 426
Capselario, 148
Çarapti, 90
Carasa, 122
Caravello, barbitonsor,
  370
Carpathio, papas, 755,
  983
Cartero, 498
Castrofilacha, 852
Cauco, 381, 686
Cauco, presbyter, 395
Cauco, presbyter, cantor
  ecclesie Crete, 858
Chandachiti, 240, 287,
  825
Chandachiti, sutor, 79
Chandaquitus, 137
Charchopulo, cerdo, 902

Mussalo, 56, 247
Mussuro, papas, 730
Musuli, 161
Musurachi, 45, 67
Musurachi, son of Costas, 216
Nigroponte, de, 774
Otobono, 551
Paço, 953
Pancalo, 588
Pantaleo, Pantalio, 564, 705
papas, 394, 514, 617, 708, 801
Paradiso, 196
Paradiso, clericus, 241
Paramandi, 167
Pascaligo, cerdo, 907
Paulo, 209
Pelecano, 767
Pendafili, 76
Pendamati, papas, 243, 569
Perdicari, 214
Petro, ienuvessus, 934
Petronicola, son of Costa, 533
Petropulo, 706
Pifani, 680
Pinaca, called Mauro, villanus, 968
Pisani, 747
Pisano, 308
    Pleiro, natural son of Marcus, 466
Ploreo, 466
Ponte, de, 381
Portu, de, 881
Prachimi, fusarius, 696
Prassino, 801
Preco, 504
Provençale, 110
Quaquo, 402
Quirino, 80, 87, 94, 215, 288, 407, 508, 615, 678, 758, 816, 864
Quirino, famulus, 190
Ragusseo, 769

Ragusio, 345
Rinaldo, de, 666
Ritio, frater, 905
Rodho, 601
Rosso, 75, 388, 734, 878
Rosso, aurifex, 240
Rosso, speçarius, 25
Rota, de la, 2
Rugerius, 852
Sabeta, wife of Rugerius, 852
Sachilari, papas, 533
Saclichi, called Caçomata, 596
Sancti, presbyter, 932
Sandala, iuparius, 787
Sanuto, 349, 819, 851
Sarandino, 560
Sarchiero, 590
Sauriano, 766
Scandolario, 220
Sclavo, 848
Sclavo, de Stampalia, 39
Sclavo, iuparius, 5
scuterius, 397
Selopulo, 25, 670
Selopulo, aurifex, 79, 304, 792
Serfioti, son of Michali, 475
Sfaco, papas, 10
Sguro, 486
Sichini da ca' Geno, 550
Siligardo, 193
Sinadino, 980
Sirigo, 700
slave, 63, 75, 172, 224, 264, 287, 324, 579, 806
Spano, 912
Spano, son of Iohannes, 912
Stadioti, 899
Sulimano, 38
Suriano, 732
Suriano, son of Hemanuel, 698
Taliapetra, 884

Taliapetra, presbyter, 723, 940
tartarus, 473
tartarus, slave, 982
Theocaropulo, called Vircto, 845
Theologo, de, papas, 310
Thocaropulo Archavli, 845
Thocaropulo, called Pothus, 845
Thocaropulo, son of Costas, 845
Tholoiti, 85
Tiepolo, 37
Tiepolo, speçarius, 682
Torcello, de, 98, 980
Torello, 893
Tricha, 141, 580, 598
Tricha, son of Iani, papas, 591
Trigrea, son of Michael, 840
Trivixano, 146
Valla, 886
Vari, 138
Vassallo, 720, 875
Vataçi, 134
Vaxalo, 195, 620
Venerio, 178, 180, 185, 680
Vergi, papas, presbyter, 115
Vestarchi, 253, 658
Vido, 95, 433
villanus, 343
Vlacho, 766
vlacus, slave, 31
Vlasse, 287
Vardali, 328
Vurgari, 222, 773
Xeriti, caligarius, 337
Xida, 669
Geracho
    Georgius, papas, 129
Geracofano
    locus, 507
Gerani

casale, 598

Gerapetra, 266
   Carbonus, prevostus, 805

Gerardina
   Cauco, daughter of
      Marcus, 30

Gerardo
   Costantius, 61
   Constançius, 815
   Costas, villanus, 447
   Georgius, villanus, 447
   Iacobus, 345
   Iohannes, notarius, 783
   Paulus, 387

Gerardus
   Bononia, de, frater, 85
   Desde, 926
   stipendiarius, 881

Gerducius
   Iacobiis, de, 781

Gerita, 338

Germanus
   Chefula, monachus, 784
   Chefala, papas, 912

Geromonacus
   Varnavas, penitencialis
   Sancti Montis Sinai, 778

Geronimo
   Corer, 932
   neno, 390

Gersora, 526

Gesse
   Hemanuel, 912
   Iohannes, papas, 612

Gici
   Georgius, tartarus, slave,
      975
   Helena, wife of Matheus,
      975
   Matheus, 975

Gidho
   Antonius, 549

Gierachari
   Nicolaus, 564

Gilbertus
   Dandulo, consiliarius, 401
   Dandulo, ducha Crete,
      123

Giorgici
   Selopulo, calogerus, 982

Girardina, 571

Girardinus
   Parma, de, 540

Girardo
   Betin, 896
   Çan, notarius, 340

Gisello
   Petrus, 328

Gisi, Ghisi, Gissi
   Agnes, wife of Marinus,
      171, 461
   Alexius, 802, 915
   Andreas, 145, 171, 172,
      352, 821
   Angelus, 186
   Anzolera, daughter of
      Iohannes, 615
   Bonuça, wife of Philipus,
      317
   Cali, 766
   Caterina, daughter of
      Marinus, 759
   Constantia, widow of
      Iohannes, 435
   Constanza, wife of
      Iohannes, 615
   Francischinus, 690
   Franciscus, son of
      Marinus, 759
   Frangula, 397
   Georgius, 758, 805, 811,
      812
   Helena, daughter of
      Andreas, 172
   Helena, wife of Marinus,
      759
   Hemanuel, 120
   Hemanuel, called
      Scopelo, 8
   Iohannes, 82, 89, 352,
      435, 577, 951
   Iohannes, called Scopelo,
      8
   Iohanninus, 615
   Laurencius, 117, 131
   Marchesina, daughter of

   Iohannes, 615
   Marco, 347
   Marcus, 189, 346, 349,
      352, 357, 362, 615,
      797
   Marcus, scriba palatii,
      341
   Maria, 172
   Marinus, 171, 186, 199,
      461, 684, 758, 805
   N., aurifex, 541
   Nicolaus, 171, 352, 437,
      758, 812, 813
   Nicolaus, son of Marinus,
      759
   Nicolaus, sutor, 766
   Palma, 927
   Peracius, 353
   Petrus, son of Hemanuel,
      120
   Philipus, 317, 347
   Potha, 8
   Quirolda, 363
   Remundinus, diaconus,
      411
   Richiolda, 430
   Robertus, 171, 352
   Stephanus, 489

Gisla, 565

Gislando
   Iohannes, 469

Gissi, see Gisi

gladium, 9

Glernu
   locus, 940

Gligoropulo
   Cali, daughter of
      Nicolaus, 685
   Nicolaus, 684
   Stamatini, 685

Gligorus
   Anafioti, mensurator, 780

Goço
   Agnes, natural daughter
      of Franciscus,
      notarius, 28
   Franciscus, notarius, 27
   Sophia, wife of

Francicus, notarius,
27
Gonçaga
Georgius de,
seneschalcus, 130
gonella, 375, 383, 404, 959
Goni
Hemanuel, papas, 904
Gorgorapti
Hemanuel, catellanus,
called, 159
Gorna
Dominicus, 514
Gornario, 408
Goro, Gorro
Andreas, 641, 655
Iohannes, 109
Mariçoli, 805
Paulus, 772
Stamati, 599
Stamatius, 75, 142, 160
Gotardus
stipendiarius, 880
Gracianus
Georgio, 760
Gracias
Granela, 950
Graciolla
Tarono, wife of Matheus,
756
Gracula
casale, 601
Gradenigo, see Gradonico
Grado
Marchesina de, 46
Gradonico, Gradenigo
Agnes, 186, 883, 957
Agnes, daughter of
Michael, 603
Agnes, soror, abbatessa,
939
Agnes, widow of Iacobus,
343
Agnes, widow of
Micaletus, 382, 432
Agnes, wife of Petrus of
Chanea, 250
Agustino, 318

Andreas, 242, 259, 415,
577
Andriola, wife of
Bertucius, 822
Angelota, widow of
Nicolaus, 185
Aniça, 158
Antonius, 285, 287, 359
Baiardus, 679
Bartholomeus, 36
Bartholomeus, doge of
Venice, 238
Benedicta, widow of
Dominicus, 232
Bertucius, 822
Cali, natural daughter of
Bertucius, 823
Cali, widow of Nicolaus,
11
Çanachius, 941
Cecilia, 924, 930, 976
Dominicus, 186, 187, 232
Dominicus, provincialis
ecclesie S. Marci,
939
Donata, 395
Egina, wife of Petrus, 778
Florentia, wife of Gabriel,
461
Fraçisci, 362
Francisca, wife of
Matheus, 431
Franciscus, 172, 185
Francus, 94
Frangula, wife of
Nicolaus, 262
Frangullus, 242
Frasenda, wife of Marcus,
209
Frosenda, 347
Frosenda, widow of
Marcus, 919
Gabriel, 461, 843
Helena, 23, 354
Hemanuel, 679, 972
Hemanuel, papas, 354
Iacobus, 27, 343, 452,
454

Iohannes, 91, 172, 326,
383, 412, 423, 946
Iohannes, ducha Crete,
512, 746, 748, 749,
752
Iohannes, naturalis, 393
Iohannes, preco, 375
Leonardus, 91, 242, 365,
492
Mafio, 994
Magdalena, 262
Magdalucia, 93
Marcus, 93, 186, 209,
241, 261, 412, 418,
702, 826, 919
Marcus, ducha Crete, 266
Marcus, de Venetiis, 242
Marcus, sartor, 128
Maria, 91, 172, 366, 242
Mariçoli, 976
Mariçoli, wife of
Andreas, 242
Matheus, 431, 855
Matheus, frater, 504
Micaletus, 382, 432
Michael, 91, 186, 378,
603, 822
Michaletus, 1, 370
Nicolaus, 11, 128, 185,
260, 262, 459, 565,
855
Nicolaus, factor, 618
Nicolaus, mensurator,
called Muglo, 374
Nicolaus, scriba, 481
Nicolaus, son of Iacobus,
27
Nicoletus, 479
Nicolota, de Rethimno,
934
Nicolota, widow of
Leonardus, 492
Petronilla, 682
Petronella, wife of
Marcus, 702
Petrus, 91, 359, 425, 778,
822, 843
Petrus, ducha Crete, 238

Petrus, frater, 504
Petrus, de Chanea, 250
Philipa, 370, 692
Salamoneta, widow of
    Andreas, 415
Salomica, widow of
    Andreas, 259
Simonetus, 924, 930
Simonetus, son of
    Iacobus, 454
Stamatius, 752
Stephanus, consiliarius,
    226, 345
Theologu, wife of
    Iohannes, preco, 375
Theolosia, wife of
    Nicolaus, 856
Titus, 242, 479
Trisu, daughter of
    Antonius, 285
Yeronimus, 425
Zanachius, 622
Gradonico Besucho
Agnes, wife of Michael,
    941
Michael, 941
Gradu
Iohannes de, 791
Marula, wife of Iohannes
    de, 791
Gramaticopulo
Dionissius, aurifex, 805,
    807
Hemanuel, 944
Herini, wife of Dionissius,
    aurifex, 807
Granella
Costa, servitor, 806
Gratiadeus, 416
Gratias, 950
Helena, wife of Gracias,
    950
Iohannes, presbyter, 416
M., 502
Nicolaus, son of Costa,
    806
Simeon, 672
Simonetus, 423

Granfiorius
Saxo, guardianus scole S.
    Marie Cruciferorum,
    441
Graphyonus, Grafeus, Grafio
Saxo, 57, 187, 233, 353,
    391, 526
Granela
N., 43
Nicolaus, 393, 824
Nicolaus, preco, 106, 337
Potha, wife of Nicolaus,
    824
Grassa
Theodora, 184
Grasso
Agnes, widow of
    Marinus, 527
Franciscus, presbyter,
    890, 894
Marinus, 527
Nicolaus, 147
Petrus, 528
Grataca, 526
Gratia
Flabia, widow of Iacobus,
    cerdo, 91
Habramo, daughter of
    Iohannes, 720
Gratiadeo
Herini tu, 797
Gratiadeus
Granella, 416
Grato
Venerio, Marcus, 463
Gratonus
Dandulo de Venetiis, 958
Grattaparte
Theodorus, 517
Greco
Antonius, 690, 806
Antonius, natural son of
    Daniel, 285
Daniel, 283
Dominicus, 65, 152, 557,
    587
Erina, wife of Antonius,
    806

Franciscus, 856
Frangulus, 806
Herigina, wife of Simeon,
    890
Marchesina, wife of
    Marinus, 250
Maria, 285
Maria, bulgara, 856
Maria, wife of Simeon,
    65
Mariçoli, widow of
    Petracius, 285
Marinus, 250, 283, 806
Marinus, natural son of
    Daniel, 285
Marula, daughter of
    Antonius, 806
Marula, widow of
    Franciscus, 856
Petracius, 285
Petrus, 516, 556, 560
Petrus, natural son of
    Daniel, 285
Richiolda, wife of Petrus,
    557, 560
Simeon, 65, 557, 890
Simonetus, son of Petrus,
    557
Greculo, Gretulo, Gretola
Caterina, widow of
    Iohannes, 731
Iohannes, 319, 531, 586,
    731
Iohannes, senex, 567
Marçoli, wife of
    Iohannes, 319
Paulus, 823
Grego
Franciscus, 942
Gregorius
Anafioti, 181
Basilino, 699
Cornaropulo, 754
Foscolo, ieromonacus,
    308
Langadhioti, 39, 281
Laudis, de, medicus,
    cirurgicus, de Spinis,

413, 420, 667
magister, 526
Maurea, 8
Smalino, de, 942
Vasilino, 697
Yesse, 227
Gretola, see Greculo
Grice
cavalleria, 210
Grifa, 146
Griffo
Marcus, prior S. Petri, 511
Grimaldena
Sophia, 730
Grimaldi, Grimaldo
Agnes, wife of
Bartholomeus de, 778
Andreas de, 703
Bartholomeus de, 456,
462, 457, 778
Bartholomeus de,
notarius, 26, 89
Dimitrius, 223
Franciscus de, 17
Georgius de, 703
Hergina de, 703
Iacobus, 26
Iohannes de, 17, 336, 703
Petrus de, 703, 779
Philipa, wife of Iohannes
de, 336
Grimani
Agnes, 968
Agnes, wife of
Bonacursius, 966
Andreas, presbyter, 125
Bo., 171
Dominicus, 335, 956, 958,
977
Dominicus, notarius,
cancellarius Crete, 24,
89, 212, 952, 953,
960, 993
Dominicus, scriba palatii,
341
Flor, wife of Dominicus,
cancellarius Crete,
961

Franciscus, 177, 666
Georgius, 792, 793
Georgius, presbyter, 293,
435
Iohannes, 556, 562, 577
Iohannes, clericus, 438
Iordanus, 164, 450, 499,
506
Le., 577
Leo, 305
Marcus, 14, 31, 195, 514,
523, 671
Marcus, piliçarius, 787
Maria, 110, 666
Marinus, ducha Crete,
198, 300
P., clericus, 569
Petrus, de Venetiis, 195
Grimano
Petrus, 671
papas, calogerus Chefala,
908
Gripiota
Helena, 26
Gripioti
Costa, preco, 912
Stephanus, 912
Gripiotissa
Agnes, 785
Cali, 452, 818
Helena, 794
Papadia, 947
Grisoni
Maria, 106
Grisovulato
Hemanuel, papas, 825
Michael, 825
Grispo
Raynaldus, 121
Grissena
Maria, 331
Grisum, grisa, 287, 590
Grita, 935
Gritola
Antonius, 897
Francus, 897
Georgius, preco, 897
Helena, daughter of

Georgius, 897
Iohannes, 943
Sophia, 897
Gritti, 682
Iacomina, 73
Xeni, 856
Grivanter
Iohannes, 540
Grucio
Thomas de, 673
Grummo
Georgius, 428
Grusi
Quirino, daughter of
Iohannes, 819
guardianus
scola S. Marie, 656
scola S. Petri, 656
guardianus Fratrum
Heremitarum, 288
guardianus Fratrum Minorum
Blasius, frater, 370
Firmo, Paulus de, 351
guardianus scole S. Marie
Cruciferorum
Saxo, Granfiorus, 441
Guarientius
Trivixano, 159
Guernioti
Cali, widow of Georgius,
604
Georgius, 604
Guido
Antonius, 409
Canale, de, 190
Iohannes, 410
Nigroponte, de, frater,
678
Valaresso, 189
Guillon
Agnes, 309
Gulialmo
Beletus, 635
Gulialmus
Piamonte, de, cerdo, 647
Sascaes, catelanus, 625
Gulicinus
Venerio, 308

Gulielma
  Milano, de, 3
Gulialmo, Gulielmo
  Sophia, 114
  Titus, presbyter, 57
  Titus, subdiaconus, 663
Guilialminus
  Catellanos, natural son of
    Iohannes, custos, 518
Guilelmus, Gulielmus
  Apmelmus, 814
  Brexiano, peliparius, 494
  Bruno, 58
  Castelo, de, frater, 408
  Cimbischi, aurifex, 588
  Clarencia, de, 192
  Elena, wife of Petrus, 402
  Ferraria, de, 683
  Ferraria, de, sartor, 351
  frater, 557
  Iacobina, daughter of
    Petrus, 402
  Iohannes, 402
  Lambrusa, de, 711
  Londonara, de, 711
  Nicolaus, subdiaconus,
    406
  Nigroponte, de, 474
  Padua, de, magister, 401
  Petrus, 402
  Sabella, widow of
    Iohannes, 402
  Selerno, da, 540
  Serepeti de Prinea, 397
  Serepeze, 456
  Sophia, wife of Petrus,
    402
  Titus, 421
  Titus, subdiaconus, 416
  Todesci, 754
  Todesco, 980
  Trivixano, 157
  Valentia, de, 743
  Vaqua, 677
  Valença, de, 711
Gulambe
  Costa, villanus, 799
  Georgius, calogerus, 799

Iani, villanus, 799
  Maria, daughter of
    Georgius, 799
  Nicolaus, villanus, 799
Gulati
  Venerio, Marcus, called,
    856
Gulimena
  Agnes, 72
Gulino
  Agnes, 100
Gulyaçena
  Sofia, 382
Gulyacinus
  Venerio, 382
Gurena, 912
Gurmotena
  Cali, 590
Gurnes, Gurnia, 674
  casale, 52, 735
  locus, 929
  serventaria, 262
Gursovergina, 838

Habatis
  Paulus de, presbyter, 444
Habramo, see Abramo
Hara
  Georgius, 80
  Hemanuel, 51
  Marcus, 80
Hauracha
  Calamino, iudeus, 215
Hebela
  iudea, 936
Helea, 605, 608
  Curtesi, iudea, wife of
    Salomon, 142
  iudea, 605, 642
  iudeus, 280
  Nigroponte, iudea, wife
    of Ellia de, iudeus,
    815
  Politi, iudea, wife of
    Alcana, iudeus, 215
Helena, 51, 90, 95, 159, 229,
  244, 269, 347, 400, 418,

461, 514, 535, 542, 565,
603, 712, 751, 799, 849,
867
Achulo, wife of
  Theodorus, 242
Alexandrena, 705
Alesandro, daughter of
  Spiradus de, 598
Alexandra, daughter of
  Sperandeus de, 26
Alexandro, de, 573
Alvirando, widow of
  Matheus, 176
Androcio, de, 53
Ania, daughter of
  Iohannes de, 991
Ania, wife of Filipus de,
  434
Avonale, daughter of
  Marcus, 195
Avonale, wife of
  Antonius, 406
Bafo, 636
Baiamonte, daughter of
  Stephanus, 230
Barbadico, wife of
  Nicolaus, de
  Venetiis, 721
Bellamore, widow of
  Nicolaus, 224
Belli, wife of Antonius,
  99
blacha, nena, 309
Boçia, 140
Bono, 21, 36
Bono, daughter of Petrus,
  327
Bono, wife of Nicolaus,
  640, 654
Bonvicina, 184
Barocio, widow of
  Andreas, 154
Calergi, 343
calogrea, 411
calogrea, daughter of
  Pasia Sancti, 415
Çangari, femina, daughter
  of Michael, 316

Herini

584, 634, 640, 642, 653, 654, 662, 773, 803, 824, 899, 927
Anata, 162
ancila, 806
Athineo, wife of Iani, 927
baiula, 337, 447, 928, 931
Belilena, 800
Beraldo, wife of Angelus, 802
Bernardo, de, 713
Bersiadena, 677
Bresiadheno, 39
Calimneadhena, 296
Calothetina, 920
Calumeadhena, 314
Candaquita, wife of Hemanuel, cilerarius, 840
Candida, de, 121
Capacino, wife of Petrus, 534
Çapani, widow of Franciscus, 159
Cardami, tu, nutrix, 746
Charadhina, 550
Chasuri, iudea, widow of Sambatheus, iudeus, 809
Chiriachudena, 710
Chisamodi, daughter of Stratigi, 953
Chrusa, called, 433
Cloni, wife of Michale, 580
Cocona, 302
Cofina, wife of Leo, fornarius, 33
Colianum, 23
Condo, wife of Iohannes, 537
Condura, 452
Coroneo, wife of Pasqualis, 951
Crenu, 298
Curadena, 675
Cursari, daughter of Hemanuel, 822

daughter of Iohannes, arcerius, 74
daughter of Rodanus, 20
diaconissa, calogrea, 351
Done, wife of Antonius de le, peliparius, 137
ex-slave, 322, 548
famula, 81, 838
Flabani, 802
Fornero, 93
Foscolo, widow of Nicolaus, 139
Gemisto, wife of Theodorus, medicus, of Constantinople, 207
Geno, 93
Gramaticopulo, wife of Dionissius, aurifex, 807
Gratiadeo, tu, 797
iudea, 167, 450, 460, 639, 642, 650, 653
Iustiniano Quença, 796
Listena, 93
Lurotomo, widow of Constantinus, papas, 304
Maçamano, wife of Philipus, 206
Mangafadhena, 48
Martuça, daughter of Hemanuel, 788
Mauroceno, 792
Mauroiani, 425
Megallomata, baiula, 110
Michael, 849
Mino, wife of Costas, 74
Miradhena, 74
Modhino, de, 48
mother of Nichitas, 51
Mudacio, widow of Iohannes, 589, 604
Muglena, 254
Muradhena, 74
Murisco, daughter of Iohannes, marinarius, 349

Musto, wife of Iohannes de, 560
Musuro, servitrix, 666
nena, 271, 418, 716, 985
Nigro, wife of Stephanus, 548
Nigroponte, wife of Iohannes de, 242
Padurachi, wife of Concionis, 948
Paliaça, 647, 665
Panercomitti, wife of Dimitrius, 388
Pantaleo, de ca', 257
Pelecano, daughter of Georgius, 767
Politissa, 302
Pulachi, 856
Quirino, wife of Michali, 953
Raguseo, 425
Riscassinavi, 431
Santi, 802
Saracenus, wife of Iohannes, 141
Scandelari, tu, 882
Sclavena, 695
Sclavo, wife of Michael, 583
Selopulena, 326
Selopulo, daughter of Nicolaus, 26
Selopulo, wife of Moscoleus, 135
serviciale, 873
servitrix, 43, 93
Sifena, 867
Siligardena, 425
slave, 9, 44, 62, 75, 81, 100, 103, 115, 139, 182, 218, 224, 225, 242, 264, 284, 307, 322, 343, 363, 390, 428, 497, 504, 514, 537, 553, 569, 587, 643, 671, 706, 756, 810, 899, 912, 930
Stadhiatissa, 564

Stadi, 700
Stavris, 614
Taliapetra, wife of Lio,
    ex-slave, 621
Thalasino, daughter of
    Iohannes, 590
Thalasino, wife of
    Dimitrius, 589
Torcello, 118
Torelo, daughter of
    Petrus, 212
Triandafilo, widow of
    Nicolaus, 253
Tricha, wife of Iani,
    papas, 590
Trivisano, widow of
    Marcus, 607
Turcho, wife of Iohannes,
    824
Turcopulina, 707
Vanichi, natural daughter
    of Fucha, 539
Varillu, 811
Venerio, 49
Viadro, 86
Vissuclena, 753
Vlastudena, 337
Vurgari, wife of Nicolaus,
    955
Vurgarina, 225
Hermolaus
    Blanco, 68
    Coppo, 829
    Minoto, 415
    Savonario, 789, 895
Heroplasa
    Quirino, widow of Petrus,
        915
Heudochia, see Eudochia
Honesta
    Carandino, wife of
        Nicolaus, 889
    Molino, de, 115
    Taliapetra, 709
Hospitale, 651, 852, 962
    domus Dei, 275
    fraternitatis, 813
    fraternitatis S. Marie, 810,

816, 845
Misericordie, de Venetiis,
    275
novum, 103, 117, 330,
    342, 344, 345, 358, 361,
    362, 366, 389, 395, 396,
    641, 645, 648, 656, 666,
    675, 682, 684, 687, 688,
    690, 692, 709, 727, 741,
    744, 746, 749, 751, 753,
    757, 806, 974
novum ecclesie S. Marie
    Cruciferorum, 700, 705,
    714, 722
novum fraternitatis S.
    Marie , 789
novum fraternitatis S.
    Marie Cruciferorum,
    724
novum fratrum scole S.
    Marie, 437
novum Latinorum, 764
novum scole S. Marie
    Cruciferorum, 68, 72,
    73, 74, 76, 80, 86, 89,
    91, 95, 107, 110, 332,
    355, 370, 440, 667
novum S. Marie, 782, 888
novum S. Marie Dei
    Genitricis, 720
novum S. Spiritus, 394,
    868, 875, 878, 882,
    890, 899, 909, 910,
    915, 920, 921, 924,
    927, 928, 930, 934
Pietade, de la, 905
scola S. Marie, 826
scola S. Marie
    Cruciferorum, 270
scola S. Spiritus, 96
SS Apostolorum Petri et
    Pauli de Venetiis,
    275
S. Antonius, 858, 859
S. Antonius pauperum,
    849, 851, 853, 854,
    856, 857, 860
S. Antonius, Spiritus

Sanctus, 838
S. Maria, 62, 315, 320,
    325, 328, 818, 994
S. Maria Cruciferorum,
    187, 257, 259, 262,
    267, 269, 270, 275,
    284, 286, 294, 296,
    298, 307, 634, 634,
    637, 645, 776, 781
S. Maria mulierum, 887
S. Spiritus, 202, 259, 266,
    267, 273, 292, 294,
    298, 392, 307, 353,
    831, 834, 965, 968,
    972, 976, 985, 987
vechio de S. Maria deli
    Crusochieri, 347
veterum, 103, 344
veterum S. Marie
    Cruciferorum, 72, 76,
    95, 928
Yerusalem, 974
Hurssa
    Cornario, 900
Hyro
    casale, 579
    episcopatus, 579

Iachopo, see Iacobus
Iaco
    iudeus, 300, 460
Iacob
    Raynerio, de, canonicus
        Calamonensis, 616
Iacoba, 162
    Bono, widow of
        Laurencius, 855
    Dadho, wife of Zaninus,
        857
    Habramo, wife of
        Nicolaus, 161
    Ragusio, wife of
        Nicolaus, 345
    Nigroponte, de, 678
    Teocari, 202
    Urso, wife of Michael,

714
Venerio, daughter of
Nicoletus, 93
Iacobellus, 664, 669
Avonale, 873
Bevardo, 216
Clugia, de, 667
Cornario, 876
Firiolo, son of Leonardus,
480
Hengelardis, son of
Bartholomeus de, 412
Lambardo, marangonus,
846
Manolesso de Venetiis,
880
Medio, de, 289
Mortagnana, 937
Urso, 584
Vassallo, 703
Vassallo, son of Marcus,
875
Vigonçia, de, 934
Iacobi
Carducius, 11
Michael, 73
Iacobicius
Pizamano, 748
Iacobina, 7, 15, 277, 619, 634,
824
Avonale, 480, 603
Barbadico, 586
Bocontolo, 863
Bono, 927
Bono, wife of
Bartholomeus, 818
Borgognono, 969
Brogognono, wife of
Marcus, 342
Calogalo, 873
Caravello, daughter of
Franciscus, 371
Catelano, 635
Clugia, wife of Iohannes
de, 449
Cornario, 204, 257
Cornario, wife of Alexius,
de domu maiori, 360

Cornario, wife of
Andreas, 360
Dondi, wife of Iohannes,
344
Dono, wife of Petrus, 637
Firmo, daughter of
Franciscus de, 46
Fodhelo, wife of
Nicolaus, arcerius, 4
Gulielmo, daughter of
Petrus, 402
Iordanino, 9
Iustiniano, 288
Longo, wife of Marinus,
482
Moço, widow of Andreas,
676
Mucio, widow of
Andreas, 230
Mussalo, 467
Quirino, 307
Raguseo, wife of Marcus,
488
Rosso, natural daughter of
Georgius, 734
Rucini, 699
Savimonis, wife of
Albertus de, ianuens,
410
Savoia, wife of Petrus de,
868
Sclavo, widow of Petrus,
656, 827
Sclença, 813
Stanchario, daughter of
Manfredinus de,
soldatus, 400
Teocari, widow of
Angelus, 258
Truli, 452
Vaxalo, daughter of
Georgius, 620
Iacobinus
Bono, 690, 732
Suriano, 599
Vassalo, 764
Iacobiis
Francisca, wife of

Gerducius de, 781
Gerducius de, 781
Iacobucius
Biaqua, 8
presbyter, 964, 968
Iacobus, 9, 472
Avonale, 593, 594
barbitonsor, 573
Baroci, 749, 979
Baroci de Venetiis, 453
Belli, 186
Blanco, presbyter, 37, 58,
73, 81, 259, 293
Blancula, iudeus, 155
Bocontolo, 56, 388, 781
Bollani, 35, 102
Bonivento, de, magister,
medicus, cirurgicus,
968
Bononia, de, frater,
bacalarus, 393
Brancha, de la, 399
Brogognono, 287
Burgundione, 515
Burin, speciarius, son of
Iohannes, de
Bononia, 393
Çampani, 902
Çamus, 419
Çancharole, 74, 668, 794
Caravella, 271, 409, 418,
473, 628
Caucho, frater, 547
Caucina, 497
Cavaro, 140
Corario, 81
Cordefer, 521
Cordeferro, 136
Corgiano, 8
Cornario, 62, 270, 290,
577, 656
Cornario, called
Maçaroni, 257, 271
Dandulo, 705
Delenda, de, 789
Diesolo, 12
Donato, 800
Dono, 752, 889

Santorini, 857
Sirici, 540
S. Herini et Thirassia, 454
Ioa
  iudeus, 200
Iocadha
  iudeus, 809
Ioachinus
  Mudacio, 166
Ioana
  Scuthi, 778
Ioanni
  Castamoniti, presbyter,
    701
Iochudas
  iudeus, 174
Iohachim
  papas, 539
Iohana, 43
Iohanachi, Iohanachius
  calogerus, 824
  Cortesano, 607
  Quirino, 608
Iohanina
  Rosso, daughter of Aniça,
    34
  Sabba, 652
Iohaninus, Iohanninus, 598
  beccarius, 456
  Filaretis, de, 62
  Franco, 132
  Geno de Venetiis, 387
  Rugerio, son of
    Constantinus de, 159
  Vido, 447
Iohannes, Çan, Çanachi,
  Zanachius, Zanaki, Zan,
  Zuan, 113, 328, 436, 468,
  482, 502, 524, 554, 559,
  570, 573, 579, 634, 654,
  662, 673, 692, 693, 697,
  799
  Abbate, de, 189
  Abbate, son of Georgius
    de, 384
  Abramo, 55
  Acardo, 108, 235, 272,
    442

Aço, 478
Acotanto de Sithya, 990
Afrato, 247, 278, 279
Agapi, 912
Albi, 600
Albi, son of Nicolaus,
  600
Alexandria, de, 268, 515
Alexandro, de, 98, 193,
  448, 559, 776, 780,
  782
Alimanus, 310
Ambelioti, 622
Amico, de, 733
Andianopolita, papas, 793
Andrianopolita, 214
Andriopuliti, 579
Ania, de, 990
Ara, 903
arcerius, 74
Avonale, 524, 534, 593,
  594
Avonale, scriba, 548
Aymo, 673, 857
Bafo, 636
Balbo, 238
Balduin, 604
Balduvino, 554
balistarius, famulus, 125
Barbarigo, 412
Baroci, 714, 749, 969,
  978
Baronci, 104
Barbadico, 14
Bartholomei a Pino, 762
Becario, 569
Becheto, 739
Becheto, comestabilis
  pedester, 117, 868
Bectaro, 578
Belegno, 622
Bellamore, de, 7, 163,
  451
Belli, 7, 11
Belli, presbyter,
  capellanus duche
  Crete, notarius, 511
Bellono, 154, 515, 521

Benedicto, 703, 711, 715,
  717, 721, 723
Benedicto, consiliarius
  Crete, 374
Bergamo, de, 711
Beto, 153, 705, 770
Bevardo, 216
blachus, 181
Blanco, presbyter, 780
Bocanigra, 34
Bolani, 12, 717
Bonaldis (Bonaudis), de,
  magister, cirurgicus,
  195, 203, 662
Bonano, 265
Bono, 36, 71, 100, 376,
  487, 683, 718, 732,
  927
Bono, notarius, 196
Bonsolo, 318, 450
Braçamonte, presbyter,
  411, 547, 548
Bradi, 257
Brexano, 404
Brexiano, presbyter, 28
Brogondiono, 609
Bruno, 774, 778
Burgundione, 515
Burgundione, son of
  Petrus, 515
Burin, de, 393
Caçochirio, 168
Cafato, papas, called
  Meçolati, 841
Calavro, 848
Calbo, 164
Caliva, 84, 619
Callopulo, papas, 955
Calomatri, 74
Calomendrino, 48
Cambaluri, 632
Çampani, 293, 294
Canale, de, 109, 139, 169,
  287
Canalo, 37
Çancarolo, 140, 538, 585,
  601, 606
Çane, 993

Iohannes

Çangaropulo, called
  Condoiani, 435
Canis, 43
Capelario, son of
  Stephanus, 617
Capella, papas, 769
Capello, consiliarius, 123
Capitalo, mensurator, 374
Capuço, 268
Carandino, 628
Carasa, 122
Caravella, 251, 259, 623
Cariti, villanus, 302
Cartofilaca, 282
Carturio, de, 470, 771
Castamoniti, 926
Castrofilacha, 852
Catellanos, custos, 518
Caterino, 298
Catidiano, 887
Cauco, 129, 262, 267,
  354, 570, 571
Cavallo, 65, 231
Çavari, 785
Çeno, 377
Çeno de Venetiis, 410
Chandachyti, 296
Cheraffa, 788
Cherchelli, 724
Cherchioli, 384
Chiliopulo, 622
Cimbischi, 610
Clarencia, de, 142
Clida, 968
Clugia, de, 449
Colona, 869, 891
Colona, senex, 873
Começano, de, 491
Condo, 537
Condo, aurifex, 466, 501
Contareno, 345
Contareno de Venetiis,
  786
Coppo de Venetiis, 914
Çordano, de, de Venetiis,
  coraçanus, 935
Cordeferro, 25
Corfioti, 39

Cornario, 75, 89, 108,
  157, 171, 206, 207,
  247, 262, 266, 308,
  312, 342, 361, 430,
  560, 618, 671, 741,
  742, 788, 819, 967-
  969
Cornario, called
  Sclavinus, 312
Cornario de domu maiori,
  62, 182, 206, 252,
  314, 643, 834
Cornario de Venetiis,
  256, 364
Cornaropulo, 208
Cortaci, 34
Curinoclissi, 860
Cursari, son of Hemanuel,
  822
Cuvoclissio, 855
Cuvuclisio, papas, 145
Dadho, 27, 254, 656
Dandulo, 201, 353, 365,
  389, 433, 679, 688,
  834, 836, 972
Dandulo, clericus, 584
Dandulo, ex-aurifex, 853
Dandulo, frater, 351
Dandulo, miles, 959
Dario, 88, 108, 226
Deo, de, clericus, 369
Desde, 259
Despelo, 574
Diaco, 287
Doce, 479
Dolce, de la, prior, 478
Dondi, 34, 36, 211, 228,
  344, 383
Dondi, peliparius, 264
Done, son of Antonius de
  le, peliparius, 137
Dono, 55, 59, 250, 337,
  346, 350, 355, 362,
  425, 587, 643, 709,
  981
Doto, son of Xenus, 581
Dragomano, 967
Dragonese, 557

Drossio, 682
Duodo, 399, 848
Enço Claudi, 489
ex-slave, 776
Faletro, 478
famulus, 540, 972
Ferraria, de, 711
Ferro, 763
Filareto, 919
Firmo, de, 60, 67, 211,
  385
Firmo, de, notarius, 207,
  925
Florencia, de, caporalis
  equester, 130
Fontanella, 331
Fosalta, de, 398
Fosculo, 199
Fradello, 153, 204, 242,
  294, 487, 562, 710,
  906
Fraganulis, de, 246
Franco, frater, 35, 194,
  249, 637
frater, 229, 959
Fucha, murarius,
  (Iacobus), 842
Fucha, villanus, 397
Furesto, 106
Furlano, 71, 588
Fuscarino, 887
Fuschi, called Perpiro,
  302
Fussiara, 746
Garguli, 865, 869, 873
Gastrea, presbyter, 208
Gavrili, 110
Geno, 258, 287, 795, 880
Geno Maurogonato, 251
Geno de Venetiis, 69
Gerardo, notarius, 783
Girardo, notarius, 340
Gisi, 82, 89, 223, 352,
  435, 577, 951
Gisi, called Scopelo, 8
Gislando, 469
Goro, 109
Gesse, papas, 612

Blancula, Eudhocia,
widow of Iacobus,
155
Calamino, Xathi, widow
of Auracha, 215
Cali, 127, 323, 445, 450,
460, 639, 642, 653,
892, 954
Caluda, 127
Çamatena, 552
Cardina, 127
Carteru, Parnatissa tu, 892
Chalocheranna, 127
Chana, 175
Charia, 200
Chasuri, Herini, widow of
Sambatheus, 809
Cherana, 459, 608, 639,
954
Cherana, called Pangalia,
widow of Ioa, 200
Chimefti, 631
Chrusafa, 608
Chrussi, 215
Cigio, 127, 595
Eloa, 653
Esther, 170
Eudochia, 141, 174, 180,
596, 821, 988
Feussini, 127
Fineta, 127
Frosini, 650
Gaudhi, Eudochia, widow
of Samargia, 142
Hebela, 936
Helia, 605, 642
Helena, 642, 653
Herigina, 167, 450, 460,
639, 642, 650, 653
Linadhena, Cali, wife of
Moyses, son of Leo,
459
Nigroponte, Hellea, wife
of Ellia de, 815
Nomico, Cali, daughter of
Samuel, 123
Nomico, Pernatissa,
widow of Samuel,

123
Pangalia, Cherana, 200
Parnatissa, 300
Plecti, 323
Plumari, Potha, wife of
Lingiachus, 445
Potha, 280, 642, 650, 653,
954
Pothiti, 300
Rodo, Parmyu, wife of
Samerya de, 892
Sabathea, 892
Samerya, Cali tu, 892
Scolarena, 988
Seta, Eudhochia tu, 127
Seti, 605
Soi, 180
Stamatini, 650
Tardina, 595
Vlimidhena, 300, 301

iudeus
Alcana, Politi, 215
Alexandria, Chavi de, 174
Alexandria, Chavi de, 174
Balbi, Iecudha, speciarius,
595
Balbo, Iacuda, 127
Balbo, Iecuda, 650
Balbo, Micali, 383
Balbo, Sambatheus, 595
Balbo, Yeremia, 127
Balbo, Ysagia, 127
Belança, Helia, 200
Blancula, Iacobus, 155
Branchio, 120
Çacha, 300, 301
Calamino, Hauracha, 215
Cali, Leo, 458
Cali, Leo, son of Moyses,
459
Cali, Moyses, son of Leo,
458
Calo, 821
Capsale, 459
Capulus, 988
Carvuni, Moyses, 155
Casani, Çacha, 988
Casani, David, 944, 988

Casani, Ligiacus, 944
Casani, Sambatheus, 988
Cermia, Lingiachus de,
650
Chagi, 200
Chasuri, Sambatheus, 809
Chavi, 174, 180
Cumaro, Samargias, 821
Curtesi, Salomon, 142
Curtesus, 608
David, 246, 716
David, de Chanea, 650,
954
Elia, 639
Elya, magister, phisicus,
127
Gaudhi, Samargia, 142
Helea, 280
Helia, 450, 460, 564
Helia, magister, medicus,
phisicus, 960
Heliachi, 155
Iacobus, teotonicus, 738
Iaco, 300, 460
Ieremia, 514
Ioa , 200
Iocadha, 809
Iochudas, 174
Lazarus, 280, 650
Leon, Rebi, 450
Ligia, 821
Lingiacus, 127, 170, 174,
200, 459, 650
Mauro, Moyses, 718
Michael, 215, 631
Michael, sacerdos, 127
Michael, Tobia, 175
Michali, 393
Missina, Iosef, 954
Mordachay, 450
Moyses, 323, 393, 605,
608, 642, 650, 653
Nacia, Vlimidhi, son of
Sambatheus, 142
Nigroponte, Ellia de, 815
Nomico, Samuel, 123
Parnu, monacus, 642, 653
Pastela, Lingiacus, 246

Laguta
  casale, 216
Lalacus, 39
Lambardena
  Aniça, 864
Lambardo
  Barbara, 864
  Georgius, 588, 968
  Hemanuel, marangonus, 846
  Iacobelus, marangonus, 846
  Iacobus, 530, 541
  Marchesina, wife of Iacobus, 530
  Marinus, corrigarius, 213
  Nicoletus, 600
Lambardus, 69
Lamber
  Çalon, Antonius, 320
Lambi
  Ianuens, 648
Lambrusa
  Guilielmus de, 711
Lamire
  Bartholomeus de le, 671
Lancaiotus
  Afano, de, 137
Lançalotus, Lanzalotus
  Ferraria, de, comestabilis pedester, 742
  Mulino, de, 437
Lançani
  Symeon, 475
Lançarotus
  Molino, de, 789
Lançe
  Messana, de, 110
lancea, 117
lanceta, 9
lancia, 9
Lando
  Marinellus, de Venetiis, 431
  Marinus, 101
  Nicolaus, 25
  Petrus, 59, 85, 238, 667
  Piero, 330

lanecum, 568
laneçus, 529
Langadhioti, Langadioti
  Georgius, 922
  Gregorius, 39, 281
  Iacobus, 281
  Iohannes, 281
  Marula, 705
  Nicolaus, 524
  Philipa, 347
  Stamatius, 281
  Vaxilius, papas, 281
Lango
  vinea, 8
Langovardena
  Aniça, 922
Langovardo, Languvardo
  Agapiti, 406
  Alexius, 659
  Costanda, 616
  Donatus, 923
  Elena, monaca, 223
  Georgius, 403, 410
  Iacobus, 590
  Mangusu, widow of Georgius, 403
  Marcus, 598
  Maria, wife of Agapiti, 406
  Minoti, wife of Nicolaus, 403
  Nicolaus, peliparius, 403
Languvardena, 835
laniçolum, 568
Lano
  calogerus, 949
Lanzalotus, see Lançalotus
Lappus
  Florentia, de, provisionatus, 737
Larani
  casale, 90
Larano
  serventaria, 478
Larcana
  feudum, 721
Larioma
  serventaria, 472

Larocha
  F. de, 479
Lathura, Latura
  Hemanuel, 52, 674
  Iohannes, 674
  Maria, sister of Hemanuel, 52
  Theodorus, 52
  Theodorus, son of Iohannes, 674
Laude, Laudis
  Gregorius de, medicus, cirurgicus, de Spinis, 413, 420, 667
Lauredano
  Georgius, scriba in camera camerariorum comunis, 847
Lauredina
  Portu, de, 717
Laurenciis
  Michaletus de, 792
Laurencio, Laurentio
  Agnes de, 867
  Augustinus de, 143
  Fina de, 917
  Georgius de, 695
  Iohannes de, 740
  Iohannes de, presbyter, 782
  Marula de, 899
  Petrus de, 993
  Petrus de, presbyter, 55, 408
Laurencius, Laurentius, 327
  Alexandria, de, 843
  Barbadico, 637, 695, 716
  Becario, 399
  Bellamore, de, 350
  Beraldo, 800
  Berardo, 221
  Bono, 855
  Caravella, 251, 468
  Caravela, 600
  Çate, 380
  Clugia, de, 502
  Dono, 647, 651, 652, 656, 673

Marcello
  Agnes, 31, 716
  Çanini, 716
  Dominicus, 672
  Georgius, 116, 264, 376,
    382, 494, 666, 672,
    716, 951
  Iohannes, 716
  Nicolaus, 59
  Nicolaus, notarius, 353
  Nicolaus, piscator, 462
  Nicoleta, wife of
    Georgius, 116
  Petrus, 59
  Philipus, 116
  Stamata, 716
Marchesina, Marchexina, 85,
    269, 290, 332, 388, 436,
    448, 453, 454, 504, 530,
    554, 570, 573, 576, 585,
    672, 746, 782, 810, 826,
    930
  Alberto, wife of Nicolaus,
    preco, 143
  Aplada, wife of Georgius,
    695
  Avonale, wife of Marcus,
    195
  Baffo, 925
  Balastro, wife of
    Franghia, 933
  Barbo, 35, 457
  Baroci, 298, 714, 749
  Baroci, wife of Iacobus,
    749
  Belli, wife of Nicolaus,
    626
  Betadena, 776
  Beto, widow of Michael,
    813
  Biaqua, daughter of Luca,
    417
  Bolani, 898
  Bonmaracadho, de, 73
  Bragadino, daughter of
    Michaeltus, 661
  Calergi, 749
  Çampani, wife of Petrus,

  293
  Canale, widow of
    Marinus de, 346
  Cartero, widow of
    Georgius, 498
  Caucho, 571
  Cauco, wife of Nicolaus,
    11
  Cauco, wife of Petrus,
    471
  Cornario, 270
  Cornario, abbatissa of S.
    Laurencius, 266
  Cornario, daughter of
    Iohannes called
    Sclavinus, 312
  Corner, daughter of
    Iohanninus, 340
  Dandulo, 689
  Daughter of Hemanuel,
    240
  Descamato, 840
  Dono, daughter of
    Nicolaus, de Sythia,
    637
  Firmo, wife of Nicolaus
    de, notarius, 505
  Gisi, daughter of
    Iohannes, 615
  Grado, de, 46
  Greco, wife of Marinus,
    250
  Habramo, widow of
    Nicolaus, 182
  Lambardo, wife of
    Iacobus, 530
  Liçardo, daughter of
    Hemanuel, 240
  Lido, widow of Iohannes,
    482
  Lulino, 284
  Magno, widow of
    Marinus, 900, 963
  Marcolena, 627
  Milano, de, 90
  Morari, daughter of
    Thomas, 321
  Pantaleo, widow of

  Andreas, 921
  Pantaleo, wife of
    Nicolaus, 551
  Pelegrini, daughter of
    Petrus, 418
  Pispola, daughter of
    Antonius, 620
  Placentia, de, 980
  Plasencia, widow of
    Nicolaus de, aurifex,
    322
  Ponte, de, 157
  Popo, 87, 89, 273
  Portu, wife of Stamati de,
    370, 691
  Ragiis, widow of
    Iohannes de, 678
  Raguseo, 801
  Raguseus, wife of
    Iohannes, 451
  Rainaldo, de, 884
  Raynaldo, de, 354
  Rucino, wife of Vasili,
    380
  Sclavo, wife of Marcus,
    598
  Sclença, 924
  serviciale, 314, 461
  Simeone, wife of
    Leotofredus, 514
  sutrix, 23
  Symeon, wife of
    Litofredus, 179
  Syssini, 254
  Tanto, widow of Marcus,
    923
  Tore, de la, 869
  Trivisano, 486
  Vasalo, 875
  Vendilino, 516
  Venetando, 248, 693
  widow of Paganucius,
    spatarius, 43
Marchesinus
  Foscari, 296
Marchesius
  Colona, 379, 380
Marchesus

Iana, tu, 835
Ippo, de, 965
Kerardo, widow of
Marcus, 810
Languvardo, wife of
Agapiti, 406
Lathura, sister of
Hemanuel, 52
Liveri, daughter of
Georgius, corrigarius,
213
Lulino, 195
Maçamurdi, 966
Macrea, ex-slave, 776
Madio, daughter of
Nicolaus de, de
Venetiis, 872
Magno, 878
Manarolo, 838
Marçani, 568
Manolesso, wife of
Laurencius, 378
Marchyano, widow of
Costas, 238
Mastoritis, 909
Mauro, wife of Iohannes,
aurifex, 884
Melissini, 29
Mello, de, 327
Mercadho, widow of
Petrus, 769
Mercato, wife of
Nicolaus, 278
Michael, wife of Thomas,
christianus, 730
Milano, de, 89, 95, 368,
675
Milea, 321, 705
Mileo, 103
Minardo, 485
Modhino, monaca, widow
of Iohannes, 797
Molino, de, 446, 826
Molino, daughter of
Benedictus de, 260
Monthechiena, 504
Moradena, da, 722
Morelo, wife of Nicolaus,

776
Moscomilena, 50
Motena, 94
Mudacio, Mudaço, 679,
776
Mudacio, widow of
Iacobus, 425
Mudacio, wife of Petrus,
20
Murisco, wife of
Iohannes, marinarius,
349
Musurachi, wife of Iani,
710
nena, 74, 542, 553, 814,
835
Nino, 179
nutrix, 749
Pagano, wife of Marcus,
cirurgicus, 813
Paleologo, 20
Pantalio, daughter of
Michali, 694
Papadia, 874
Papadia Metupa, widow
of Nicolaus, papas,
970, 983
Paradisa, 934
Paramandi, widow of
Georgius, 167
Pasqualigo, 714
Pasqualigo, daughter of
Dimitrius, de
Nigroponte, 774
Pasqualigo, nena, 687,
921
Pellecanissa, 96
Pendamatena, 243
Peracio, 740
Periptera, 281
Piçamano, wife of
Nicolaus, 54
piçocara, daughter of
Franciscus Goço, 28
Placencia, widow of
Franciscus de, 250
Politena, 257
Pollitissa, 710

Ponte, de, 89, 94
Prebrissa, 243
Provatu, 469
Pseludhena, 466
Pullodermatena, 698
Quirino, 23, 368, 687,
699
Quirino, daughter of
Petrus, 491
Quirino, daughter of
Philipus, 4
Quirino, wife of
Amoratus, 455
Quirino, wife of
Iohannes, 819
Quirino, wife of
Leonardus, 358
Rapacino, 991
Raptrea, 282
Rogena, 746
Romanitissa, 549
Rugerio, wife of Iohannes
de, 158, 569
russa, slave, 692
Sachlichi, 296
Saclichi, widow of
Georgius, called
Caçomata, 596
Salonicha, slave, 240
Salonichea, 777
Sancti, 754
Sanuto, 700
Scandolario, 160
Scandolario, widow of
Andreas, 555
Scarpantho, de, 833
Schinoplocho, 801
Sclavena, 524
Sclavo, daughter of
Antonius, 657
Sclavopula, 383
Sclavulina, 855
Sclença, daughter of
Iohannes, 515
Segnolo, 294
Selopulo, wife of
Georgius, aurifex,
304

Selu, 724

serviciale, 380, 511, 878, 901

servitrix, 35, 48, 78, 79, 344, 364, 663

Sinori, baiula, 776

slave, 15, 17, 35, 39, 72, 81, 98, 100, 124, 165, 172, 224, 264, 284, 294, 361, 358, 366, 370, 425, 452, 465, 480, 492, 500, 504, 508, 514, 529, 629, 636, 692, 722, 756, 759, 829, 852, 853, 859, 875, 878, 887, 891, 905, 940, 982, 986

Smirnea, 370

Spagnolo, 8

Stadioti, wife of Georgius, 900

Staurachi, 220

Stepaliotissa, 796

Suriano, 156, 649

Suriano, wife of Georgius, 733

tartara, slave, 719, 720, 727

Thalasino, daughter of Iohannes, 604

Theofilopulo, calogrea, 689

Tonano, wife of Nicolaus, frenarius, 513

Toscano, 443

Traversario, 419

Trignan, widow of Angelus, 787

Trivisano, wife of Nicolaus, 129

Trivixano, widow of Guilelmus, 157

Tronena, 35, 57

Turmiti, de, 869

Vaçangena, 670

Vanichena, 965

Vardali, wife of Georgius,

329

Vardalina de Calessia, 98

Vardhena, 466

Varuchena, 316

Vasmuli, wife of Nicolaus, 534

Vassalo, 716

Vassalo, daughter of Iulianus, 20

Vassalo, widow of Riçardus, 422

Vassilichi, 94

Vaxalo, 620

Vaxalo, natural daughter of Andreas, 620

Venerio, 327, 366, 429

Venerio, daughter of Iohannes, 110

Venetando, wife of Iohannes, 104

Vercia, slave, 343

Vergici, 791

Vetula, 746

Vidho, tu Leo, 558

villanula, 987

Vincentia, widow of Adam de, 421

Vlasto, widow of Syphus, 210

vulgara, slave, 391

Xemoni, 330

Yesse, daughter of Iohannes, 227

Maria Magdalena ecclesia, 179

Mariça, 931

Mariçoli, Marçoli, Marcioli, Maricioli, 79, 225, 233, 269, 328, 411, 417, 427, 474, 482, 514, 552, 568, 634, 635, 644, 667, 689, 697, 764, 883, 965

Acre, wife of Leonardus de, 212

Albi, 90

Albi, daughter of Nicolaus, 600

Androcio, 124

Armin, wife of Çanachi, 783

Avonale, daughter of Antonius, 407

Balbi, wife of Dardius, 247

Baldu, 888, 974

Barbadico, wife of Marcus, 553

Baxilio, 162

Beto, 701

Betto, wife of Marcus, 309

Bolani, 35

Bolani, wife of Andreas, 898

Bono, 927, 939

Brexiano, 105

Burgundione, natural daughter of Marcus, 515

Canale, wife of Iohannes de, 139

Çangisti, daughter of Petrus, aurifex, 614

Caravello, daughter of Georgius, barbitonsor, 370

Caravello, daughter of Iacobus, 473 629

Catelan, 845

Cauco, 745, 746

Contarini, 360

Corario, 106

Corario, widow of Marcus, 80

Çordanino, wife of Nicoletus, 490

Cornario, 225, 290, 689, 772

Cornario, daughter of Iohannes called Sclavinus, 312

Cornario, wife of Andreas, 250, 257, 331

Corner, 339

Çustignan, 931

Serfioti, wife of Michali, 475

Maripetro
Agnes, 275
Andreas, 275
Marcus, 275

Marmaia
Michael, de Tartaro, 287

Marmara
Nicolaus, 389

Marmari
Georgius, papas, 47

Marmatra
Eudhochia, wife of Xenus, 537
Xenus, 537

Marmora
Georgius, papas, 798
Georgius, slave, 224

Marnelus, 835

marner
Quirin, Manoli, 677

Marollus
Pixano de Venetiis, 786

Marota, 478, 686, 692, 724
pauper, 714

Marreta
Bolan, wife of Franciscus, de Venetiis, 843

Martha
Chyriacopulina, formerly Maria, now, monaca, 191
Monaca, 254, 784
Turcho, wife of Iacomo, 905

Martino
Bartholomeus de, 474
Hemanuel, 987
Iohannes de, 144, 631

Martinus
Bortolo, presbyter, 627
Pilia, 869
Sclavo, 656
Soldan, de, marangonus, de Venetiis, 936
Vicentino, 489

martone, 130

Martuça
Cali, widow of Hemanuel, 788
Erini, daughter of Hemanuel, 788
Hemanuel, 788

Martura
Helena, widow of Marcus, 508
Marcus, 508

Maru, 337

Marudalena
Bonohomo, widow of Marcus, 408

Marula, 427, 428, 710, 751, 796, 826, 827, 842, 930, 931
Adhrani, 931
Afrato, 279, 924
Ania, wife of Iohannes de, 990
Armachi, wife of Hemanuel, 69
Astimdena, 939
Bollani, wife of Thomas, 717
Brogondione, 927
Burgondione, sister of Petrus, preco, 49
Çachariadena, 939
Calergi, 835
Canal, daughter of Nicolo da, 389
Canale, daughter of Georgius de, 242
Castrofilacha, wife of Dominicus, 851
Cavalcante, daughter of Dominicus, 273
Chafatena, 946
Cherchelli, wife of Iohannes, 724
Chisamodi, daughter of Stratigi, 953
Cornario, bastard of Nicolaus, 969
Cornario, daughter of Marcus, 267

Cornario, wife of Michael, 848
Cura, tu, 705
Dandulo, daughter of Nicolaus, 972
daughter of Theodora, 61
Durente, 854
famula, 812
Formarici, daughter of Stephanus, 439
Gavra, daughter of Nicolaus, 381
Geno, soror, 982
Gradu, wife of Iohannes de, 791
Greco, daughter of Antonius, 806
Greco, widow of Franciscus, 856
Ialina, daughter of Antonius, 223
Ialina, wife of Michael, 248
Langadioti, 705
Laurentio, de, 899
locus, 821
Marangoni, 224
Massaro, daughter of Dimitrius, 894
Mauro, 982
Milano, daughter of Iohannes de, 89
Militibus, daughter of Bartholomeus de, 584
Morgano, 116
Mosco, wife of Georgius, piliparius, 908
Mudacio, 880
Mudacio, widow of Matheus, 928
Musselle, daughter of Georgius, 801
Mussalo, daughter of Georgius, 56
Mussuro, wife of Iohannes, cerdo, 713
Pantalio, 692

Pantalio, wife of Andreas,
941
Pefani, 40
Petenario, wife of
Nicoletus, 838
Pramatepti, de, 35
Puli, 869
Quirino, 716
Rimano, natural daughter
of Maximus de, 44
Rinaldo, daughter of
Georgius de, 666
Sancti, wife of
Thomasinus, 677
Saxo, daughter of
Grafeus, 391
Secreto, 292
Secreto, daughter of
Paulus, 343
servitrix, 649
Spano, 912
Taliapetra, daughter of
Petrus Bualli, 353
Vala, 851, 930
Venerio, 395, 716, 811,
974
Venetiano, wife of
Franciscus, 902
Venier, 716
vidua, 640, 654
Maruliano
Potha, 876
Marulu
Cali, 107, 716
Marviara, 327
Masaço
Iohannes, marangonus,
called, 566
Masarno
Nicolaus, 382
Masaro
Antonius, 405
Marçoli, wife of Antonius,
405
Nicolaus, 110
Masia
Climiti, 869
Masientano

Iohannes, 15
Philipa, daughter of
Iohannes, 15
Masiis
Nicolaus de, 444
Masochopo
Theodorus, 516
Masocopina, 316
maspilum, 469
Masragas
papas, 849
Massari
Iohannes, 785
Massario
Dimitrius, 744
Massaro
Aniça, 894
Dimitrius, 894
Marula, daughter of
Dimitrius, 894
Massimus
monacus, 52
Massochilena
Sophia, 466
Massuri
Iohannes, 784
Mastoritissa
Maria, 909
Masu, 103
Masuse
Climantino, de, 108
Masvisa
Enço Claudi, daughter of
Iohannes, 489
matalinus, 649
mataracium, mataratum, 121,
422, 516, 529, 701
Mategaru
Papadia, 820
Mater Domini, called Smileo
ecclesia, 947
Mathea, Mathia, 693, 710
Baroci, natural daughter
of Iohannes, 749
Contarino, 931
Cornario, 257, 267
Mudacio, 888
Mudacio, wife of

Frangulius, 973
Pantalio, wife of Marinus,
frenarius, 644
Matherelo
Bertucius de Venetiis,
531
Çanina, wife of Bertucius
de Venetiis, 531
Matheo
Cali tu, 701
Matheus, Mathio, 915
Abramo, 866
Agapito, son of Andreas,
39
Alvirando, 176
Berino, 548
Clugia, de, clericus, 54
Cordeferro, 25
Cutaioti, 471
Doto, 581
Furlano, 688
Gavra, papas, calogerus,
680, 784
Geço, 820
Geno, 20, 547
Gici, 975
Gradonico, 431, 855, 994
Gradonico, frater, 504
Lucari, 731
Mantelo, de, presbyter,
878
Milano, de, 90
Mocenigo, 806
Montello, de, presbyter,
341, 384, 675, 701,
917, 919, 921, 928,
929, 964
Mudacio, 223, 928
Mudacio, natural son of
Petrus, 31
Mudacio, natural son of
Petrus, Castrum
Themenensis, 31
Pelecano, 912
Pola, de, presbyter, 578
Quirino, 182, 777
Quirino, son of Nicolaus,
298

Raguseo, 879
Rosso, 857
Rota, son of Georgius de
    la, 2
Taiapetra, 586
Taliapetra, 368, 621, 861,
    911
Tarono of Venice, 756
Turco, 840
Valla, 195
Venerio, 275, 279
Matia, see Mathea
Matono
    Agnes, 541, 705, 909
    Andreas, 541, 845
    Georgius, 232
    Iacobus, 184
    Nicolaus, 229, 231, 845
    Thomasina, wife of
        Nicolaus, 229, 231
Matotenena
    Agnes, 957
Matra
    Hemanuel, villanus, 720
Matricho, 930
Matriera
    Thefanu, 497
Maufredo
    Mariçoli, 871
    Michaletus, 870
    Potha, 871
Maura, 425
Maurachi
    Chostancius, 948
Maurea
    Gregorius, 8
Maurica
    Costas, 933
    Hemanuel, 953
Mauro
    Agnes, 269
    Agnes, widow of
        Thomasinus, 515
    Andreas, 592
    Antonius, 153, 166,
        301, 811
    Bartholomeus, 16, 153
    Caliça, daughter of

Iohannes, 108
calogerus, 720
Chatarucia, wife of
    Thomas, de Venetiis,
    855
Cherana, 588
[...], consiliarius Crete,
    123
Donatus, ducha Crete,
    760, 762, 952
Franciscinus, 836
Georgius, villanus, 720
Iohannes, 108, 402, 767
Iohannes, aurifex, 864,
    884
Iohannes, bastasius, 870
Marcus, 150, 151, 237,
    471, 566
Maria, wife of Iohannes,
    aurifex, 884
Marula, 982
Moyses, iudeus, 718
Nicolaus, 46, 67, 614,
    885, 950
Pinaca, Georgius,
    villanus, 968
Stadhiati, Michael, called,
    564
Thomas, de Venetiis, 855
Thomasina, 465
Thomasinus, 515
Mauroceno
    Agnesina, wife of
        Lodovicus, 762
    Antonius, 762
    Caterucia, 379
    Cataruça, daughter of
        Michaletus, 356
    Cristina, wife of
        Antonius, 762
    Çufredus, ducha Crete,
        660
    Franciscus, de Venetiis,
        355
    Herini, 792
    Iohannes, 767
    Iohannes, ducha Crete,
        472

Iohannes, son of Michael,
    79
Laurencius, 275
Lodovicus, capitaneus
    Crete, 762
Lucia, wife of
    Michaletus, 355
Mafio, 355
Marcus, 258
Marcus, consiliarius
    Crete, 56, 812
Marinus, 393
Marinus, consiliarius
    Crete, 78
Marinus, ducha Crete,
    237, 333, 362, 725
Marinus, aurifex, 79
Michael, 79
Michaletus, 355
Nicolaus, 245, 618
Nicolotus, 806
P., 637
Piero, 355
Rambaldus, 959
Richiolda, widow of
    Marcus, 258
Thomas, 393
Maurogonato
    Geno, Andreas, 854
    Geno, Iohannes, 251
Mauroianena
    Xeni, 236
Mauroiani
    Herini, 425
    Nicolaus, 287
Mauromati
    Iohannes, 398, 631, 771
    Michael, 268
Mauropulo
    Nicolaus, 697, 967
Maurus
    frater, 99
maxelarium, 181, 207
Maximus, 838
Meço
    Marcus de, 905
Meçolati
    Cafato, Iohannes, papas,

Mediolano, Iohannes de, 740
Mescato
    Heudochia, 909
Mesina
    Michael de, 620
Messana
    Franciscus de, 816
    Georgius de, 754
    Iohannes de, 291
    Lançe de, 110
    Michael de, 78
    Michael de, speçarius, 191, 201
    Nicolaus de, 291
    Potha, wife of Lançe de, 110
    Zeffaludi, de, frater, 120
Messarea, 210
Messena
    Iohannes de, 727
Mesina
    Çanachius de, 832
    Georgius de, 832
Messopanditissa
    ecclesia S. Titi, 89
Metachara
    Michiel, villanus, 987
Metachieristi
    Antonius, 528, 589
    Cali, 588
    Leo, 523, 528, 581, 588
Metaxa
    casale, 212
    locus, 864
Metupa
    Costas, 970, 983
    Gabriel, son of Costas, 970
    Iohannes, 628
    Iohannes, papas, 18
    Luca, 970, 983
    Maria Papadia, wife of Nicolaus, papas, 970, 983
    Michael, son of Costas, 970
    Nicolaus, papas, 49, 283,

966, 970, 983
Stamati, papas, 667
Stamatius, 214
Miani
    Christina, 930
    Stephanus, 249
Micael, see Michael
Micale
    Capadocha, papas, 784
    Dimitropulo, 940
Micaletus, Michaletus
    Barbarigo, 412
    Cornario, 833
    Cornario, nobilis vir, 834
    Fontana, de la, 399
    Gradonico, 382, 432
    Misina, de, 861
    Quirino, 396
    Simitecollo, son of Michaletus, 477
    Toscano, subdiaconus, 429
Micali
    Balbo, iudeus, 383
    Clomidhi, 311
    Thocaropulo, called Vilius, 845
Micaliçi, 314
Micaliçius, 649
    Cornario, 871
    famulus, 397
Micelivus
    marangonus, 502
miçellum, 315
Michael, Micael, 29, 257, 273, 631, 633, 770, 814, 984
    Abbate, de, 803
    Albanis, de, 102
    Andentiis, de, spatarius, 611
    Andradhino, 622
    Andreas, 696
    Androcii, specialis, 674
    Angelidhi, papas, 467
    Antonius, de Venetiis, 937
    Aplada, 927

Balbo, 650
Barbadico, 973
Barbo, 466
Benedicto, 98
Beta, 275
Beto, 696, 814
Blico, 318
Bonacorsso, 942
bordonarius, 107
bulgarus, slave, 298
Calderero, 563
Calomati, 74, 987
Çangari, 316
Çaninus, 959
Carandino, 237
Carasa, 122
Caravella, 250, 296
Caravello, 300
Catamano, papas, 517
Caterina, widow of Nicolaus, 274
Caucho, 548
Chandachyti, arcerius, 305
Chanioti, 655
Charchia, 287
Charcomata, 254
Chrispina, 275
Chrusolura, 189
Clydone, de, spatarius, 612
Comita, 892
Comnino, 797
Corento, de, slave, 242
Cornario, 270, 848
Coroni, 199
Çusto, clericus, 424, 434
Damiano, 76
Despotato, de, 205
Dochanos, 522
Dominicus, consiliarius Crete, 56, 78
Doto, son of Xenus, 581
Erini, 849
Exotrocho, 279
Fafuna, papas, 771
famulus, 712
Fasuli, 119

Thomasinus, 439, 812
Moroni
Andreas, 693
Mortagrana
Iacobellus, 937
Moscalis
Selopulo, 25
Moscana, 181, 724, 801
ancila, 143
Anglidhi, widow of papas
Michael, 467
Avala, 159
baiula, 585
Bono, 677
Cuçupa, nena, 826
Francho, widow of
Nicolaus, 574
nena, 799
nutrix, 746
Parapsomachina, 513
Theologiti, nena, 838
Varsalu, 466
Moscata, 428
Mosco
Agnes, daughter of
Georgius, peliparius,
908
Dominica, daughter of
Georgius, peliparius,
908
Georgius, papas, 798
Georgius, peliparius, 908
Helena, daughter of
Georgius, peliparius,
908
Marula, wife of Georgius,
peliparius, 908
Moscoleo, Moscoleus, 697
Hemanuel, 45, 47, 48, 52,
53, 73
Medio, de, 877, 879, 883
Selopulo, 135, 670, 792
Sirigo, 586
Moscomilena
Maria, 50
Moscomili
Costas, 50
Georgius, 50

Leo, 50
Moscona
Iohannes, 126
Moscu
Suriana, 766
Mostaci
Baroci, wife of Marcus,
446
Motena
Maria, 94
Moti
Michal, papas, 784
Mothono
Cali de, 147
Movathi
Caterina, monaca, 777
Moyses, 650, 653
Cali, iudeus, son of Leo,
iudeus, 458
Carvuni, iudeus, 155
iudeus, 323, 393, 605,
608, 642, 650, 653
Mauro, iudeus, 718
Mozenigo
Petrus, ducha Crete, 401
Mt Marmaro
Antonius de, 447
Nicolinus de, 447
Mt Sinai
ecclesia, 466, 538, 539
iconomus monasterii, 681
monache, 431
monasterium, 18, 50, 63,
64, 316, 541, 604,
727, 751, 759, 852
ordo grecorum, 527
Mt Sion, 916
Mucio, Muçio
Agnes, 677
Agnes, wife of Angelus,
592
Angelus, 592
Cali, 48, 94
Iohannes, 521
Marcus, 197
Mudacio, Mudaço, 83
Antonius, 107, 307, 365,
389

Augustina, 337
Bernardus, 956
Cali tu, 706
Caterina, natural daughter
of Petrus, 223
Dimitrius, scutiferus, 294
Elena, widow of Petrus,
223
Francisca, wife of
Antonius, 365
Franciscus, 3, 223, 252,
342
Frangulius, 914, 973
Georgius, 753
Helena, daughter of
Antonius, 107
Hemanuel, 971
Herigina, daughter of
Pauletus, 110
Herini, widow of
Iohannes, 589, 604
Iacobus, 20, 210, 223,
252, 425
Ioachinus, 166
Iohannes, 21, 37, 365,
425, 428, 438, 589,
604, 776
Iohannes Bicho, 352
Iohannes, clericus, 440
Iohannes, diaconus, 442
L., presbyter, 637
Luca, presbyter, frater,
canonicus, 57, 442
Marçoli, 425
Marcus, 30, 138, 336,
425, 583, 622, 756,
776
Maria, 679, 776
Maria, widow of Iacobus,
425
Maria, wife of Petrus, 20
Mariçoli, 37
Marula, 880
Marula, widow of
Matheus, 928
Matheus, 223, 928
Matheus, natural son of
Petrus, 31

Matheus, natural son of
  Petrus Castrum
  Themensis, 31
Mathia, 888
Micheletus, 880
Michelinus, 240
Nicolaus, 643
Parlatus, 623
Petrus, 629, 956, 971
Petrus, discipulus, 583
Petrus, frater, 182, 309,
  447, 452, 469, 485
Nicoletus, 358
Parlatus, 8
Pauletus, 110, 577
Paulus, 148
Petrus, 20, 68, 138, 210,
  223, 365, 412, 442
Petrus, called Parlatus, 30
Petrus, frater, 23, 182,
  309, 447, 452
Rosa, wife of Marcus, 776
Stamatius, 955, 991
Zanakius, de Venetiis, 756
Mudacio Bicho
  Iohannes, 956
Mudaço, see Mudacio
Mude
  Marcus, 987
Muglena
  Herini, 254
Muglo
  Gradonico, Nicolaus,
    mensurator, called,
    374
Mulia
  casale, 57
Mulida
  Georgius, 964
  Hemanuel, 927, 964
  Pasqual, villanus, 927
  Stamatinus, villanus, 927
Mulino
  Anniça de, 745
  Antonius de, clericus, 558
  Cali, natural daughter of
    Marcus de, 746
  Frangulius de, 745

Hemanuel de, 745
Lançalotus de, 437
Lodovicus de, 746
Marcus de, 746
Marcus de, preco, 549
Ursula de, 746
Mundas
  Dolfin, 83
Mundeo
  Nicolaus de, caligarius, 6
Munega
  Beriola, 356
murarius
  Bertus, 465
  Cauco, Petrus, 180, 792
  Cornario, Antonius, 110
  Firmo, Marcus de, 78
  Ialina, Michael, 78
  Lino, Iohannes, 38
  Locassio, Iohannes, 26
  Milano, Iohannes de, 152
  Pasqualis, 388
  Petraca, Petrus, de
    Venetiis, 166
  Sarmea, Alexius, 891
  Sclavo, Nicolaus, 768
  Tarte, Costa, 770
  Trivisano, Iohannes, 565
  Vidho, Marcus, 432
  Vituri, Antonius, 708
Murgano
  Iohannes, 346, 360, 362
Murgeliani, 833
Murgo, see Amorgos
Muricicho
  Bartholomeus, presbyter,
    845
Murisco
  Herini, daughter of
    Iohannes, marinarius,
    349
  Iohannes, marinarius, 349
Murtaro
  Theodorus, 287
Musco
  Panerimiti, Dimitrius, de,
    303
Muscole

Nicolaus, 129
Musget, 165
Musolena, 643
Mussale, Mussalo
  Blasius, 190
  Callus, 802
  Calos, 56, 101
  Georgius, 56, 169, 232,
    247, 801, 802
  Iacobina, 467
  Iohannes, 56, 190, 232,
    247, 801, 807
  Leo, 42, 283
  Marula, daughter of
    Georgius, 56, 801
  Michael, 820
  Micheletus, 795
  Sophia, widow of
    Georgius, 801
  Sophia, wife of Georgius,
    56
Mussgeta
  Georgius, 570
  Nicolaus, 157
  Stamatius, 287
Mussele
  Leo, 101
Mussioti
  Constantinus, papas, 197
Mussovergi
  Constantinus, called
    Pigadhioti, 47
Mussuria
  Xenus, 939
Mussuro
  Anicia, 658
  Constantinus, 200
  Constantinus, papas, 139,
    153, 156
  Georgius, papas, 730
  Hemanuel, de Xurolea,
    614
  Iohannes, cerdo, 713
  Marula, wife of Iohannes,
    cerdo, 713
  Nicolaus, 45
Musto
  Herini, wife of Iohannes

de, 899

Panterio, 252

Papada
baiula, 974

Papadia, Papadhia, 835
Antonia de, 746
Cali, of S. Dimitrius, 296
Chaleucena, 262
Gripiotissa, 947
Luludhena, 931
Maria, 874
Mategaru, 820
Siropulo, wife of
Nicolaus, papas, 965
slave, 218, 242
Sophia, 874, 912
Vergicena, 337

Papadopula, Papadhopulo
Andreas, 622
Çaninus, 987
Potha, 542

papatu
Orso, Nicolaus, presbyter,
candhyanus, 417

Papadopulo
Manoli, 390

papas
Agapito, Hemanuel, 537,
544
Amurgino, Nicolaus, 386
Andianopulita, Iohannes,
793
Andreas, 207, 617
Andreas de S. Demitrio,
18
Andrianopoliti,
Constantinus, 138,
223, 281, 542
Andrinopoliti, Vasilius,
984
Andronicus, 698, 966
Angelidhi, Michael, 467
Blachernitis, Dimitrius de,
212
Çachus, 773
Çaco, Nicolaus, 695
Cafato, Iohannes, called
Meçolati, 841

Callopulo, Iohannes, 955
Calopti, Georgius, 603
Capadoca, Andreas, 891
Capadhoca, Hemanuel, 10
Capadocha, Micale, 784
Capella, Iohannes, 769
Carofilati, Michali, 507
Carpathio, Georgius, 755,
983
Castamoniti, Nicolaus,
calogerus, de
Rethimo, 925
Catamano, Michael, 517
Chefala, 894
Chefala, calogerus, 871
Chefala, Germanus, 912
Cherchelli, Nicolaus, 98
Cherianus, 802
Chirissolura, Nicolaus,
680
Chortaci, Georgius, 607
Chrussolura, Georgius,
163, 188
Chrussolura, Hemanuel,
212
Chrussolura, Vaxilius,
181, 299
Chrusoveloni, Nicolaus,
144
Chyriacus, 240
Cicandilo, Constantinus,
207
Constantinus, 593, 595
Constantinus de Chera
Pissiotissa, 18
Corinthio, Bartholomeus,
monacus, 341
Cortaci, Andronicus, 697
Costa, 796
Curtalo, Andreas, 149
Curtichi, Stephanus, 39
Cuvoclisio, Iohannes, 145
David, 695
Dimitrius, 542
Fafuna, Michael, 771
Filadelfino, Constantinus,
207
Filathropino, Nicolaus,

877
Filareto, Michael de, 468
Fochianus, 984
Gastrea, Thomas, 208
Gavra, Matheus,
calogerus, 680, 784
Georgius, 394, 514, 617,
708, 801
Georgius de Theologo,
310
Geracho, Georgius, 129
Goni, Hemanuel, 904
Gosse, Iohannes, 612
Grimano, calogerus,
Chefala, 908
Grisovulato, Hemanuel,
825
Hemanuel, 287
Ialina, Nichiforus, 599
Ialina, Petrus, 159
Iesse, Hemanuel, 613
Iohachim, 539
Iohannes, 57, 240, 281,
486, 542
Lacherinchosti,
Hemanuel de, 11
Lago, Michael, 149
Lucas, 18, 514
Lurotomo, Constantinus,
304
Macrimali, 49
Macrimale de Chira
Chosti, 18
Manoliti, Georgius, 214
Marano, Michael, 900
Marcus, calogerus, 681
Marmari, Georgius, 47
Marmora, Georgius, 798
Mastagas, 849
Mecopa, Nicolaus, 116
Metupa, Iohannes, 18
Metupa, Nicolaus, 49,
283, 966, 970, 983
Metupa, Stamati, 667
Michael, 114, 542
Michael de lo Cristo, 514
Michali, 695
Mosco, Georgius, 798

cavallaria, 177
locus, 929
Parvisio
Ugocinus de, 231
Pascale
Bono, 607, 608
Sclença, 13
Pascaligo, Pasqualigo
Agnes, 687
Agnes, widow of
Laurencius, 921
Agnes, wife of Marcus,
986
Angelus, 869
Antonius, 423
Çanin, son of Iacobus, de
Venetiis, 994
Caterucia, wife of
Marinus, 687
Caterina, wife of Fantinus,
de Venetiis, iudex
proprii, 659
Çusamana, wife of
Antonius, 423
Dimitrius, de Nigroponte,
773
Fantinus, 86
Fantinus, de Venetiis,
iudex proprii, 659
Francisca, 714, 976
Georgius, cerdo, 907
Helena, wife of Georgius,
cerdo, 907
Iacobus, 644
Iacobus, de Venetiis, 993
Iacobus, son of Dimitrius,
de Nigroponte, 774
Iacomina, wife of
Fantinus, 86
Iohannes, 409, 687
Laurencius, 686, 687, 921
Laurencius, nobilis vir de
Venetiis, 902
Marcus, 687, 986
Maria, 714
Maria, daughter of
Dimitrius, de
Nigroponte, 774

Maria, nena, 687, 921
Marinus, 496, 686
Marinus, aurifex, 808
Marinus, de Venetiis, 842
Nicolaus, 391, 687
Nicolaus, de Venetiis,
714
Placentia, 509
Sandro, son of Iacobus,
de Venetiis, 994
Torcello, de, 702
Zoana, de Venetiis, 842
Pascalius
Bono, 572
Paschalinus
Dondi, 553, 556
Pascasi
Mariçoli, piçocara,
daughter of Nicolaus,
284
Nicolaus, 262
Pascasio
Mariçoli, 31
Pascelicena
Barbadico, 916
Geno, Barbara, 924
Pascha
Fosulo, 939
Pasia
Sancti, 415
Pasqualigo, see Pascaligo
Pasqualis
Bono, 335
Busignore, de, 128
Coroneo, 951
Coroni, 388
Dondi, 559
F., de Torcello, 385
Marinus, 385
Militibus, de, 584
Mulidha, villanus, 927
murarius, 388
Sclença, 325, 530
Torcello, de, 355
Pasquasi
Marçoli, 343
Passigarius
Ugonus, 153

Passalites
serventaria, 337
Pastela
Cali, wife of Lingiacus,
246
Lingiacus, iudeus, 246
Paterimudhena
Cali, 590
Patermo
Hemanuel, 544
Paterno
Petrus de, 412
Paternoster, 331, 469
Patra
casale, 403
Franciscus de, 845
Patracensis
Iohannes, 271
patriarcha Constantinopolis,
860
Pauleta
Çampani, daughter of
Franciscus, 488
Longo, 504
Rippa, de, 194, 295
Pauletus, 552
Dono, natural son of
Petrus, 638
Habramo, 183
Mudacio, 110, 577
Quirino, 215
Pauli
Marcus, 526
Paulina, 504
Paulo
Agnes, 158
Agnes, widow of
Thomas, 675
Agnes, wife of Thomas,
417
Anna, daughter of
Philipus, 611
Antonius, 675
Francisca, 417
Georgius, 209
Helena, daughter of
Petrus, 54
Helena, wife of Petrus,

Maçamano, 206
Malpes, 817
Marcello, 116
Mengolo, 197, 443
Milano, de, 90, 94
Mioli, 563
Paulo, 124, 457, 611
Pisani, 747
Orso, 527
Quirino, 4, 461
Rippa, de, 194, 229, 295
Sanuto, 460
Savonaro, 404
Signolo, 776
Spano, son of Iohannes,
    912
Tore, de la, 113
Udene, da, 711
Vera, 601
Viaro, 577
Vigoncia, de, 210, 291,
    347, 691, 919, 966
Vitale, 57
Zigerdoti, de, 393
Phisicus
    Elya, iudeus, magister,
        127
    Fano, Thomas de,
        magister, 126
    Fredericus, magister, de
        Tredento, 25
    Helia, iudeus, magister,
        medicus, 960
    Mt Gultela, Iohannes, de,
        magister, 306
    Victor, magister, 662
    Vido, medicus, magister,
        333
Phymia
    Malvasiotissa, 769
Piamonte
    Antonius de, 711
    Filipa, wife of Gulialmus
        de, cerdo, 647
    Frangula, wife of
        Antonius de, 711
    Gulialmus de, cerdo, 647
Piçalo

Eudochia, daughter of
    Paulus, 279
Paulus, 279
Piçamano
    Herigina, wife of
        Nicolaus, 53
    Nicolaus, 53
Picamili
    Pantaleo, Andreas, called,
        857
Pichino
    Iacobus, 117
Piçina
    Barbo, Nicolaus, 404
piçocara
    Agnes, 705
    Agnes, daughter of
        Minoti, 35
    Antonia, 662
    Biera, 814
    Cali, 262
    Colona, Frangula,
        daughter of Iohannes,
        869
    Cornario, Ysabeta, 291
    Goço, Maria, daughter of
        Franciscus, 28
    Herigina, 891
    Pascasi, Mariçoli,
        daughter of Nicolaus,
        262, 284
    Lucia, 418
    Venetanda, 814
Piçolo
    Agnes, 627
    Nicoleta, 692
    Nicolota, 332
    Petrus, notarius, 500
pictor
    Benedictus, 148
    Petrus, de Venetiis, 765
    Quirino, Nicolaus, 497
pictura, 279, 548
Piçuni
    casale, 838
Piero, see Petrus
Pifaça, 548
Pifani

Georgius, 680
Piffanius
    Amurgino, son of Xeni,
        769
Pigadhulia, Pigaidulia
    locus, 47
    SS Apostoli, 240
    territorium, 101
Pigi
    casale, 108
pignata, 937
pignatarius
    Michael, 148
Pignatello, Pignatellus
    Ni. de, magister, 351
    Nicolaus, magister, de
        Brundusio, 805
pignolatum, 183, 243, 284,
    306, 984, 985
Pigoço
    Aniça, widow of Iacobus,
        273
    Franciscus, 821
    Iacobus, 273
Pilatus, 149
Pilia
    Martinus, 869
Piliçaria
    Buaeda, 380
Piliçarius
    Grimani, Marcus, 787
Pilicer
    Angelus, 579
    Marcus, 571
piliçonum, 288
piliparius, see peliparius
Pilliça
    Antonius, piscator, 38
    Vendramus, 672
Pillicena, 488
    Theodora, 38
Piloso
    Antonius, 470
    Çaneta, widow of
        Marcus, 242
    Marcus, 242
Pinaca
    Georgius, called Mauro,

Iacobus, 417
planis, 781
Plasu
    Corner, wife of
        Iohanninus, 339
Plati
    Cali, tu, 49, 283
Plecti, 730
    iudea, 323
Pleiro
    Georgius, natural son of
        Marcus, 466
    Marcus, aurifex, 466
Plemenu
    vinea, 228
Plethi, 516
Pleti, 542
Pliça
    Iacobus, 860
Pliti, 475
    ancila, 262
    Cavatorta, widow of Leo,
        29
    nena, 716
Plitibus
    Michael de, 804
Ploreo
    Cherana, daughter of
        Georgius, 466
    Georgius, 466
    Hemanuel, son of
        Georgius, 466
    Marinus, 690
    Michael, de Chanea, 79
Plubino
    Mariçoli, widow of Paulus
        de, 883
    Paulus de, 883
plumaçum, plumacium, 524,
    640, 654, 796
Plumari
    Lingiachus, iudeus, 445
    Mardachay, iudeus, 650
    Potha, iudea, wife of
        Lingiachus, iudeus,
        445
pneumaticus
    Theostirictus, calogerus,

708, 894
Pola, Polla
    Hemanuel de, 983
    Herina de, 869
    Leonardus de, 95
    Matheus de, presbyter,
        578
    Nicolaus de, presbyter,
        687, 972, 983
    Nicolaus de, scriba, 831
Polemissa
    casale, 268
    serventaria, 268
Polifengo, 208
Poliocto
    Nicolaus, diaconus
        grecus, 849
Polis
    Franciscus de, 719
    Iohannes de, 719
    Nicolaus de, de Venetiis,
        618
Politena
    Maria, 257
Politi, Polliti
    Alcana, iudeus, 215
    Antonius, 517
    Fillartus, 517
    Helia, wife of Alcana,
        iudeus, 215
    Iohannes, 517
    Nicolaus, 517
    papas, 695
Politissa
    Cali, 833
    Herini, 302
    Maria, 710
Pollo, Polo
    Çian, 962
    Contarino, 931
    Corer, 931
Poluça, 905
Ponta
    Hemanuel de, 727
Ponte
    Çanachi de, 510
    Dominicus de, 89, 90, 94,
        622

Donatus de, 616
Georgius de, 381
Iacobus de, 382
Iohannes de, 588, 590,
    592, 593, 600
Marcarius de, presbyter,
    925
Marchesina de, 157
Marcus de, 48, 50, 55, 61,
    63, 75, 87, 89, 94,
    109, 438, 615, 620,
    622
Maria de, 89, 94
Michael de, presbyter,
    929
Nicolaus de, 479, 726
Nicoletus de, 382
Petrus de, 67
Philipa, widow of
    Georgius de, 381
Popo
    Blanda, 87
    Blonda, 478
    Dominicus, 87, 89, 95,
        478
    Iohannes, 87, 89, 478
    Marchesina, 87, 89, 273
    Violenda, 87, 89, 478
Porchorum
    ruga, 121
Porco
    Iohannes, 621
    Margarita, 965
    P., 631
Porta
    Albertus da la, 954
    Bertus de la, 747
    Caterina, wife of
        Hemanuel de la, 212,
        670
    Frangulus de, 554
    Hemanuel de la, 212, 914
    Leonardus de la, 212
    M. de la, 446
    Marcus de la, 305
    Michael de, 518
    Nicolota, daughter of
        Leonardus de la, 212

portarius
    Trivisano, Michael, 319
Porto
    Donatus de, 8
    Iacobus da, 573
    Marçoli, da, 347
    Michalis de, 26
    Zan da, 347
Portono
    Daniel da, 711
Portu
    Agnes de ca', 302
    Andriolus de, 882
    Cali de, ex-slave, 692
    Çanachius de, cerdo, 882
    Donatus de, 302, 500, 813
    Georgius de, 881
    Hemanuel de, 880, 903,
        973
    Herigina, wife of
        Stamatius de, 881
    Iohannes de, 500, 591,
        674, 881
    Lauredina de, 717
    Magdalucia, daughter of
        Stamatius de, 882
    Marchesina, wife of
        Stamati de, 370, 691
    Marçoli de, 692, 881
    Morisina de, 500
    Nicolaus de, 302, 606,
        813
    Paulus de, 220
    Petrus de, 45, 46, 50, 55,
        175, 510, 555, 567,
        571, 612
    Stamati de, 370, 691, 692,
        881
    Thomas de, 220, 717, 886
Portus
    Bartholomeus de, 32
    Thomas de, 500
Poschiera
    Vivianus, 599
Possoleme
    monasterium, 284
Potami
    Iacobus, 986

Iohannes, 614
Potha, 189, 191, 250, 514,
    574, 624, 642, 650, 653,
    724, 953
    Abbate, widow of
        Iohannes de, 189
    Alimussi, wife of
        Theodorus, 768
    Bevardo, wife of
        Iohannes, 216
    Cafurena, 296
    Calergi, 506
    Çampanena, 992
    Canale, widow of
        Hemanuel de, 527,
        605
    Canea, de, 643
    Cauco, wife of Nicolaus,
        11
    Cavusi, 296
    Chandachiteno, 39
    Cumessareas, tis, 94
    Çurlopula, 281
    Dandulo, widow of
        Hemanuel, 88
    Gisi, 8
    Granela, wife of
        Nicolaus, 824
    Habramo, 885
    iudea, 280, 642, 650, 653,
        954
    Marchiani, 767
    Maruliano, 876
    Maufredo, 871
    Mergerena, 705
    Messana, wife of Lança
        de, 110
    nena, 928
    Papadopula, 542
    Pisano, wife of Michael,
        307
    Plumari, iudea, wife of
        Lingiachus, iudeus,
        445
    Rivena, 542
    Sameadena, 891
    Segredho, wife of
        Iohannes, ex-slave,

779
    Sichiachi, 873
    Simitecollo, wife of
        Michaletus, 477
    slave, 39
    Stefanachi, tu, 776
    Taliapetra, 852
    Tarachina, 469
    Trichadhena, 604
    Tuchana, 588
    Zampani, 856
Pothas
    iudeus, 174
Pothiti, Pothity, 431
    Bono, daughter of
        Stephanus, notarius,
        543
    Foscari, widow of
        Marchesinus, 296
    iudea, 300
    Quirino, wife of Paulus,
        55
Pothus
    iudeus, 600
    Thocaropulo, Georgius,
        called, 845
Prachimi
    Agnes, wife of Georgius,
        fusarius, 696
    Georgius, fusarius, 696
    Stamata, daughter of
        Georgius, fusarius,
        696
Praghanena
    Agnes, 948
Pramatepti
    Marula de, 35
Prasino, Prassino
    Cherana, widow of
        Michael, 146
    Georgius, 801
    Michael, 146
    Praxia, monaca, widow of
        Georgius, 801
Praxia
    Prassino, monaca, widow
        of Georgius, 801
pre, see presbyter

Prebrissa
  Maria, 243
preco, 577
  Alberto, Nicolaus, 143
  Burgondrone, Petrus, 49
  Cremona, Marinus de, 497
  Camulo, Georgius, 948
  Desso, Filipus, 403
  Framarino, Laurentius, 952
  Garçeti, Benedictus, 413
  Georgius, 504
  Goro, Marcus, 234
  Gradonico, Iohannes, 375
  Granela, Nicolaus, 106, 337
  Gripioti, Costas, 912
  Gritola, Georgius, 897
  Mulino, Marcus de, 549
  Quirino, Manoli, 855
  Scordili, Michael, 852
  Segredho, Michael, 783
  Torcelo, Raphael, 588
  Trivisano, Antonius, 24
preco curie Crete
  Venerio, Bartholomeus, 463
preponiscus
  Iohannes, presbyter, 316
presbyter, pre
  Acardo, Nicolaus, 215
  Albiço, Antonius, 66, 646
  Antonius, 420, 427, 557
  Antonius, cantor S. Titi, 273
  Armicha, Nicolaus, 944
  Baldagno, Dominicus de, 125
  Baroci, Petrus, 749, 821
  Baselio, Nicolaus, 57, 61, 69, 814
  Basilius, capellanus S. Tito, 343
  Baxilio, Nicolaus, 273
  Baxillo, Antonius, 696
  Belli, Iohannes, capellanus duche Crete, notarius, 511

Blanco, Iacobus, 37, 58, 73, 81, 259, 293
Blanco, Iohannes, 780
Bocontolo, Marinus, 93, 671
Bogtolo, Martinus, 627
Braçadoro, Dominicus, 414
Braçamonte, Iohannes, 411
Brexiano, Antonius, 683, 896
Brexiano, Iohannes, 28
Brixiano, Antonius, 274
Çafredo, Nicolaus, 781
Cambonus, Marcus, capellanus, 316
Castamoniti, Ioanni, 701
Castro, Raymundus de, 819
Cauco, Georgius, 395
Cauco, Georgius, cantor ecclesie Crete, 858
Cavalcante, Marcus, 89, 272, 415, 478
Dalmario, Nicolaus, 272
Dandulo, Petrus, capellanus ecclesie Crete, 428
Dandulo, Petrus, notarius, 195, 205, 412
Dimitrius, 455
Donçorçi, Marcus, 866
Donne, Petrus de le, 293, 574
Firmo, Iacobus de, capellanus S. Tito, 54, 193, 246, 568
Floravans, 25
Floravans, capellanus, 548
Fosculo, Marcus, 306, 394
Foscolo, Pantalucius, 479
Fragenes, Andreas, 214
Franciscus, 701
Fratres Predicatores, 324
Fuschi, Andreas,

archidiaconus, canonicus gerapetrensis, 663
Fuscolo, Andreas, 469
Fuscolo, Pantalinus, 409
Fuscolo, Pantalucius, 429
Gastrea, Iohannes, 208
Georgio, Dominicus, 352, 953
Granella, Iohannes, 416
Grasso, Franciscus, 890, 894
Grimani, Andreas, 125
Grimani, Georgius, 293, 435
Gulielmo, Titus, 57
Habatis, Paulus de, 444
Iacobucius, 964, 968
Iacobus, 43, 242
Iohannes, preponiscus, 316
Iusto, Michael, 209, 987, 989
Laurençio, Iohannes de, 782
Laurentio, Petrus de, 55, 408, 574
Maçamurdi, Iohannes, 918, 925, 928-930, 933, 966
Mallasaca, Georgius, 57
Mantelo, Matheus de, 878
Marçangelo, Antonius, 683
Marino, Iacobus de S. Nicolao de Scaragatore, 402
Mediolano, Donatus de, 853
Megano, Hemanuel, 784
Melissino, Nicolaus, 544
Mengolo, Petrus, 195, 285, 394
Michael, capellanus, 603
Miegano, Hemanuel, 786
Milano, Donatus de, 893, 922, 938
Milovani, Bartholomeus,

236
Montello, Matheus de,
341, 384, 675, 701,
917, 919, 921, 928,
929, 963
Mudacio, L., 637
Mudacio, Luca, frater,
canonicus, 57, 442
Muricicho, Bartholomeus,
845
Mussuro, Constantinus,
papas, 153, 156
Natalis, Iohannes, 421
Natalis, Marcus, 200
Nicolaus, 306
Nicolaus, capellanus, 519,
547
Nicolaus, capellanus
Castri Belvidere, 402
Nicolicius, capellanus,
530, 544
Nigroponte, Iohannes de,
195, 256, 273, 293
Nigroponte, Iohannes de,
capellanus cretensis,
408, 419, 664
Orso, Nicolaus, papatu et
candhyanus, 417
Paganuci, Iacobus, 574
Pantaleo, Andreas, 256,
259
Pantaleo, Antonius, 441,
705, 720, 898, 901
Pantalucius, 415
Paulo, Iohannes, 751, 921,
957
Pelegrino, Nicolaus, 675,
919, 965
Petracha, Marcus, 489
Pispola, Nicolaus, 982,
986
Placencia, Marcus de,
634, 676, 909
Pola, Matheus de, 578
Pola, Nicolaus de, 687,
972, 983
Ponte, Marcarius de, 925
Ponte, Michael de, 929

Proscarino, Donatus de,
487
Quirino, Petrus, 653
Radulfo, Nicolaus, 483
Raudo, Nicolaus, 411
Riço, Antonius de, 182,
420
Rodo, Antonius de, 57
Romano, Nicolaus, 256
Rosso, Andreas, 858
Rosso, Iohannes, 115
Rubri, Iacobus, cantor
cretensis, 412
Sancti, Georgius, 676,
932
Sanuto, Nicolaus, 858
Sclavo, Iacobus, 402
Sclença, Iohannes, 220,
751, 924
Scordili, Hemanuel, 945
Silvestro, Iohannes, son
of Petrus, 195
Simenachi, Dominicus,
917
Staurachi, Iohannes, 381,
964
Sulimani, Iohannes, 420
Taliapetra, Georgius, 723,
940
Terra, Andreas de, 822
Theodorus, 617
Toscano, Michael, 442
Traversario, Iohannes,
578
Travarsario, Sançoni, 95,
686, 909, 923
Traversario, Iohannes,
179
Trivisano, Nicolaus, 227
Trivisio, Thofanus de,
940
Ubertis, Paulus de, 57
Urso, Nicolaus, 568
Valdagno, Dominicus,
796
Venetiis, Donatus de, 940
Vergi, Georgius, papas,

115
Verona, Iohannes de, 33,
413, 671
Zeniese, Franciscus, 901
Zeniex, Franciscus, 877
Prestrie
Pollo, 83
pretor
Apochafcho, Alexius,
839
provinciale ecclesie S. Marci
Gradonico, Dominicus,
939
Prevosto
Andreas, 260
prevostus Gerapetre
Carbonus, 805
primichirius
Iohannes, 911
primicyrius S. Marci
Cornario, Philipus, 741
Primogeni
Iohannes, villanus, 968
Prinea
Serepeti, Guillelmus de,
397
Priolis
Iacobus de, 379
prior
Bononia, Andreas de,
frater, 393
Dolce, Iohannes de la,
478
Griffo, Marcus, frater, S.
Petri, 511
procuratores S. Marci, 496
Promondini
Cherana, 724
Pronicadhena
Cali, 784
Prosper
liber, 274
protopapas, 966
Provatu
Maria, 469
Provençale
Georgius, 110
Nicolaus, 489

provincialis
  Leonardus,
    archiepiscopus, 327
  Fratres Predictores, 98
provisionatus
  Florentia, Lappus de, 737
Psalatho
  liber, 949
Psatha
  casale, 831
Psefistis
  Iohannes, 542
  Leonardus, 542
Pseludhena
  Maria, 466
Psimeni
  Chieli, 545
Psiruchi
  Antonius, 514
  Bartholomeus, 233
  Helena, daughter of
    Nicolaus, 179
  Helena, widow of
    Antonius, 514
  Nicolaus, 69, 179, 514
Psolachi
  Iacobus, 141
Psomopulla
  casale, 361
Pubuna
  Venetando, Nicolaus, 208
puela
  Aniça, 924
puerulus
  iudeus, 460
Pulachi
  Erini, 856
Puladha
  Marcus, curator, 225
Puladhena, 29
Puli
  Marula, 869
Pulladi
  Costas, 710
Pullodermatena
  Maria, 698
Pulvinari, 508
pumater, pumatum, 9, 466,

527, 529

Quaquo
  Georgius, 402
Quença
  Iustiniano, Herini, 796
Quilla
  Iohannes de la, 711
Quirino, Quirin
  Agnes, 869
  Agnes, daughter of
    Marinus, 84
  Agnes, widow of Marcus,
    652
  Agnes, wife of Georgius,
    758
  Agnes, wife of Iohannes,
    453
  Amoratus, 455, 977
  Andreas, 86, 93, 234,
    334, 364, 368, 396,
    835, 914
  Andreas, de Venetiis, 333
  Andriola, daughter of
    Petrus, 73
  Angelus, 235, 280, 307,
    351, 397, 672, 774,
    778, 787, 892, 894
  Angelus, christianus, 771
  Aniça, 900
  Antonia, 73
  Antonius, 73
  Aurumplasa, 343
  B., 22
  Baldus, consiliarius, 365
  Bampaninus, 927, 977
  Bampamius, son of
    Amoratus, 456
  Bartholomeus, 18, 518
  Bartholomeus,
    consiliarius, 226, 345
  Beata, 81, 94
  Beata, daughter of
    Georgius, 288
  Beata, wife of Dominicus,
    394
  Benedetto, 333, 932

  Benedictus, 281, 683
  Benedictus, son of
    Amoratus, 456
  Bertucius, 333
  Bertucius de Venetiis,
    364
  Beruça, 551
  ca', 951
  Cali, daughter of Manoli,
    86
  Cali, de ca', now
    Catafigi, monaca,
    140
  Campagnola, 347
  Campagnola, widow of
    Andreas, 234
  Çanachius, 707
  Çanachi, comadador, 333
  Çanicha, 709
  Çaninus, 798
  Carlo, 334
  Caterina, 307, 343, 430
  Caterina, widow of
    Marinus, 915
  Caterina, wife of
    Angelus, christianus,
    771
  Chaterucia, 838
  Cherana, wife of Leo,
    beccarius, 655
  Constancia, vetula, 916
  Constantia, widow of
    Angelus, 307
  Cornarola, wife of Petrus,
    838
  Costancia, 81
  Costinus, 746
  Daniel, 84, 269
  Daria, wife of Andreas,
    333
  Daria, wife of Paulus,
    460
  Dimitrius, papas, 877
  Dominicus, 52, 100, 358,
    368, 394, 396
  Donatus, 95
  Elena, 305
  Elena, daughter of

Quirino

Benedetto, 932
Elena, wife of Iohannes, spatarius, 491
Elena, wife of Marinus, 82
Fantin, 333
Francisca, wife of Matheus, 182
Frangius, 838
Frangulla, 307
Frosini, wife of Nicolaus, 73
Georgius, 80, 87, 94, 215, 288, 407, 508, 615, 678, 758, 816
Georgius, famulus, 190
Helena, 80, 292, 397
Grusi, daughter of Iohannes, 819
Hemanuel, 55, 215, 461
Hemanuel, natural son of Paulus, 55
Hergina, 746
Herichiolda, widow of Philipus, 461
Herigina, daughter of Iohannes, 125
Herini, wife of Michali, 953
Heroplasa, 915
Heroplasa, widow of Petrus, 915
Iacobina, 307
Iacobus, 215, 240, 508
Iacomina, 86
Iani, 362
Ieronimus, 383
Iohanachius, 608
Iohannes, 125, 221, 308, 447, 453, 478, 563, 615, 757, 787, 819, 893, 915, 953
Iohannes, spatarius, 491
Laurentius, 86, 359, 362
Leo, beccarius, 655
Leonardus, 358, 368, 396, 467
Madalucia, daughter of Dominicus, 396

Mafio, son of Paulus, 83
Manoli, 86
Manoli, marner, 677
Manoli, preco, 855
Marçoli, widow of Benedictus, 683
Marcus, 64, 171, 235, 280, 297, 376, 448, 531, 652, 672, 824, 856, 919, 949
Margarita, daughter of Piero, 362
Margarita, wife of Laurentius, 362
Maria, 23, 368, 687, 699
Maria, daughter of Petrus, 491
Maria, daughter of Philipus, 4
Maria, widow of Leonardus, 358
Maria, wife of Amoratus, 455
Maria, wife of Iohannes, 819
Mariçoli, 86, 927
Mariçoli, widow of Bampaninus, 977
Marina, sister of Marinus, 83
Marinus, 81, 82, 83, 221, 298, 343, 380, 418, 915
Marinus, de Venetiis, 914
Marinus, son of Nicolaus, 298
Marula, 716
Matheus, 182, 777
Matheus, son of Nicolaus, 298
Micaletus, 396
Michael, 410, 709
Michael, spatarius, 491
Michael, sutor, 584
Michali, 953
Namoratus, 551
Ni., 351
Nicolaus, 514, 678, 684,

699
Nicholeto, called Turin, son of Marinus, 84
Nicolaus, 22, 68, 73, 81, 86, 298, 307, 308, 359, 362, 452, 778, 787, 845, 900
Nicolaus, called Turin, 82
Nicolaus, pictor, 497
Nicoleto, natural son of Paulus, 83
Nicoletus, 82, 774
Nicoletus, son of Amoratus, 456
Oreplasa, daughter of Marinus, 84
P., 632
Pe., 643
Pantalucius, 21, 231, 358, 368
Pauletus, 215
Paulus, 23, 55, 82, 297, 460, 818
Paulus, rector Rethimi, 994
Petrus, 22, 73, 86, 171, 190, 297, 444, 447, 452, 491, 535, 587, 806, 838, 899, 915
Petrus, clericus, 94, 416
Petrus, presbyter, 653
Petrus, of Venice, 68
Philippa, sister of Marinus, 83
Philipa, wife of Petrus, 22
Philipus, 4, 461
Piero, 333
Pothiti, wife of Paulus, 55
Riçardo, 334
Romeus, 190, 447
Sabeta, widow of Marcus, 856
Sofia, 397, 796
Stamatius, 690, 845
Tavian, 333
Thomado, 334, 363
Thomas, 85, 396
Thomas, frater, 92, 259,

290, 456, 656
Thomasina, 73, 172, 183,
    460
Zanaquius, 869
Zane, 333
Quirolda
    Gisi, 363

Rabi
    Peres, iudeus, 141
Raça, 671
    Petrus, 212
    Theodorus, 577
Radiseo, 373
Radulso
    Nicolaus, presbyter, 483
Regeracius
    Rugerio, de, 951
Ragiis
    Iohannes de, 678
    Marchesina, widow of
        Iohannes de, 678
Ragono
    Nicolaus de, 268
Raguseo, Ragusia
    Caliça, wife of Marcus,
        168
    Cecilia, widow of
        Federicus de, 187,
        556
    Donatus de, 233
    Francischinus, son of
        Iohannes de, 909
    Federicus de, 187, 556
    Franciscus de, 257
    Georgius, 345, 769
    Herini, 425
    Iacoba, wife of Nicolaus,
        345
    Iacobina, wife of Marcus,
        488
    Iacobus, 449
    Iohannes de, 234, 909
    Malgarita, daughter of
        Franciscus, 257
    Marchesina, 801
    Marcus, 168, 488

Margarita de, 234
Marinus, 502
Matheus, 879
Michael de, 156, 160,
    188, 233, 938
Nicolaus de, 201, 203,
    345
Nicoletus de, 233
Petrus, 641
Stamatini, daughter of
    Marinus, 502
Thomas, 879
Thomasina, widow of
    Michael, 938
Veneranda, 879
Raguseus
    Iacobus, 451
    Marchesina, wife of
        Iohannes, 451
Ragusia, see Raguseo
Ragusio, see Raguseo
Rainaldus
    Firmo, de, clericus, 809,
        815
    Marchesina de, 884
Rambaldus
    Mauroceno, 959
Ramella
    Franciscus, 69
    Marcus, 652
Ramerius
    Sanctis, de, 858
raminum, 9, 29, 529
Rampani
    Marcus, 640, 654
    Marinela, 919
Ranerio
    Anatalinus de, 627
    Blasius de, 423
    Dominicus de, 50, 327,
        406
    Franciscus de, 635
    Marcus de, 423
    Margarita, daughter of
        Franciscus de, 635
    Margarita, widow of
        Blasius de, 423
    Stamatina, wife of

Anatalinus de, 628
Rani
    locus, 722
Ranucius
    Geno, 387
    Geno de Venetiis, 774
Rapacino
    Maria, 991
    Petrus, 534
Rapalo
    Leonardus de, ianuens,
        263
Rapani
    Cali, widow of
        Theodorus, 640, 654
    Caterina, wife of
        Iohannes, 521
    Flora, widow of Iacobus,
        572
    Iacobus, 572
    Iohannes, 521, 562
    Marcus, 236
    Theodorus, 640, 654
Raphael, 552
    Baxilio, 184
    Bononia, de, aurifex, 467
    Dusano, 486
    frater, 26, 89
    frater, minister Fratrum
        Minorum, 249, 290
    Habramo, 62, 183, 196,
        302, 350, 799
    Natale, 417, 594, 595
    Natale, son of Iulianus,
        603
    Romano, sartor, 324
    Romello, 41
    Torcelo, preco, 588
Raphyolena
    Mariçoli, santola, 242
raptrea
    Helena, 20
    Maria, 282
Rasmus
    Trivixano, 484
Raudo
    Nicolaus, presbyter, 411
Ravasio

Iacobus de, 281
Ravichus
Dema, castellanus, 120
Raymundus
Castro, de, presbyter, 819
Raynaldo
Blanco, 677
Marchesina de, 354
Raynaldus
Grispo, 121
Raynerio
Dominicus de, 475
Franciscus de, 505
Iacob de, canonicus
Calamonensis, 616
Marcheta, wife of
Franciscus de, 505
Marcus de, 173
Recardinus, see Ricardinus
rector Rethimi
Quirino, Paulus, 994
Redulfus
Todesco, 203
Regina, 481
Bragadino, wife of
Michaletus, 661
Dono, 492
Geno, 30
Petacio, daughter of
Thomas, 665
Venetando, wife of
Nicolaus, 678
Vicentia, daughter of
Antonius de, 518
Regio
Tomas de, 376
Regouradho
Nichitas, 26
Remerius
Malgarita, wife of Petrus,
176
Petrus, of Venice, 175
Remundinus
Gisi, diaconus, 411
Renaudena
Agnes, 20
Renauldi
Agnes, 568

Rethimo, 8, 354, 859, 925,
993
Bafo, Andreas, 273
Castamoniti, Nicolaus,
papas, calogerus, 925
Gradonico, Nicolota, 934
Reto, 475
Rica, 15
riçalium, 959
Riçardi
Antonius, decanus
Cretensis, 412
Ricardia
servitrix, 618
Ricardinus
Arimino, de, 738
famulus, 398
Riçardo
Quirin, 334
Riçardus
Vassalo, 422
Ricele
castrum, 121
Richiolda, Richioldi, 553, 586
Caucho, 571
Calergi, 715
Contareno, 814
Cornario, widow of
Andreas de domu
maiori, 833
Cresencetio, de, 974
Gisi, 430
Greco, wife of Petrus,
557, 560
Mauroceno, widow of
Marcus, 258
Pantaleo, 814
Quirino, widow of
Philipus, 461
Rubin, wife of Marcus,
568
Secreto, wife of Iohannes,
284
Riçi
Iamicus, 121
Riçio
Donatus, 760
Luchina, wife of Donatus,

760
Padua, de, 117
Riço
Antonius de, presbyter,
182, 420
Cali, daughter of
Nicolaus de, 16
Dominicus, 805, 808
Donatus, 983
Hergina, 706
Iohannes de, 19, 351
Luchina, wife of Donatus,
983
Marculinus, 647
Marcus, 646
N. de Venetiis, 502
Nicolaus de, 16
Nicolota, 19
Venier, 338
Riçolinus
Açonibus, de, de
Tarvisio,
comestabilis
equester, 398
Riçu
Fra., 502
Riema
serventaria, 969
Rigaçus
Molino, de, 920
Rigucius, 531
Macharelo, 568
Rigus
Lisi, 597
Rimano
Balducius de, 44, 59, 85
Cali, mother of Balducius
de, 85
Franciscus de, 44, 59, 85
Franciscus, son of
Balducius de, 85
Marula, natural daughter
of Maximus de, 44
Maximus de, 44
Paulus de, 44, 60
Thomas de, 540
Rinaldo
Andreas de, 666

Georgius de, 666
Marula, daughter of
    Georgius de, 665
Rini
    Bertin, de, 347
    Calena, 994
    wife of Lorenço, 83
Ripa, see Rippa
Riparius
    Albertinus, 6
    Brogognono, Petrus, 279
Rippa
    Andreas de, 194, 229, 295
    Bartholomeus de, 193,
      295
    Blasius de, 215
    Blasius de, magister, 662
    Çaneta, wife of
      Bartholomeus de, 193
    Francus de, 194
    Natalis de, 194, 229, 295
    Nicolaus de, 950
    Nicolaus de, de Venetiis,
      872
    Pauleta de, 194, 295
    Philipus de, 194, 295
Ripus
    Thocharopulo, Costa,
      called, 845
Riscassinavi
    Herini, 431
Risticho
    Facius de, 120
Ritio
    Georgius, frater, 905
Riva
    Blasii, Blasius de, 105
    Blasius de, 45, 64
Rivena
    Potha, 542
roba, 9, 469
Robertus
    Bonsignor, de, 121
    frater, 120
    Gisi, 171, 352
Rodanus, 20
Rodhe
    Benvegnutus de, 540

Petrus de, magister, 540
Rodhi, 540
Rodhiani
    calogrea, 542
Rodhopulo, 601
Rodio
    Michael, 181
    Nichitas, 181
    Theodora, wife of
      Nichitas, 181
Rodo, Roddo, 520, 579
    Antonius de, presbyter, 57
    Dimitrius de, 854
    Georgius, 601
    monacha, 466
    Nicolaus, speciarius, 990
    Parmyu, iudea, wife of
      Samerya de, iudeus,
      892
    Samerya de, iudeus, 892
Rodolofo, Rodulfo
    Angeliera, wife of
      Iohannes, 465
    Antonius, 318, 538
    Iohannes, 465
    Sevasti, widow of
      Symeon, 539
    Symeon, 539
    Todesco, 822
Rodovano
    Michaletus, 758, 887
Rogena
    Maria, 746
Rogerio
    Antonius de, 8
    Franciscus de, 985
    Palma, wife of Petrus de,
      977
    Petrus de, 977
    Rogerius de, 8
Rogerius
    Cordeferro, 24
    Rogerio, de, 3
Rolandus
    Dadho, 776
    Natale, 71, 74
Roma, 274, 275, 328, 994
    Nicolaus de, 638

Schota de, 413
Romagnolo
    Margarita, 675, 734
    Margarita tu, 700, 878
Romana, 327
Romanitissa
    Maria, 549
Romano
    Antonius, 679, 909, 972,
      985
    Claredia, wife of
      Raphael, sartor, 324
    Galacius de, 521
    Lorenço, 336
    Marcus, 635
    Nicolaus, 180
    Nicolaus, presbyter, 256
    Raphael, sartor, 324
    Stephana, soror, 324
Romello
    Caladia, widow of
      Raphael, 41
    Raphael, 41
Romeo
    Michael, papas, 904
Romeopulo
    Helena, daughter of
      Nicolaus, 753
    Nicolaus, 752
Romeus
    Faletro, 261
    Quirino, 190, 447
Ronçini
    Iacobus, 421
Rondo, 374
ronzaleum, 738
Rosa, 39
    Canale, natural daughter
      of Marcus de, 287
    Cherana, 786
    Mudacio, wife of Marcus,
      776
    Secreto, 18
    Venetando, mother of
      Iohannes, 105
Roselli
    Donatus, 561
    Nicolaus, 561

roseta, 960
Rosselo
    Costas, 8
    Thomas, 8
Rossetus
    Cremona, da, 711
Rosso
    Andreas, presbyter, 858
    Aniça, 34
    Aniça, wife of Georgius,
        240
    Anna, 738
    Antonius, 115
    Cali, 717
    Diesolo, Leo, auxilator,
        773
    Dominicus, 100, 376
    Georgius, 75, 388, 734,
        878
    Georgius, aurifex, 240
    Georgius, speçarius, 25
    Helena, 74, 878
    Hemanuel, 74
    Iacobina, natural daughter
        of Georgius, 734
    Iacobus, 94
    Ianulius, 240
    Iohannes, 41, 75, 94, 102,
        240, 254, 428, 441,
        772
    Iohannes, presbyter, 115
    Iuliana, 34
    Marçoli, widow of
        Dominicus, 376
    Matheus, 857
    Michaletus, preco, 804
    Nicolaus, 34, 409, 613
    Nicoleta, daughter of
        Dominicus, 376
    Nicolaus, frater, 656
    Petrus, 74, 210, 254, 316,
        376, 579, 658
    Sophia, 94
    Soy, wife of Michaletus,
        preco, 804
    Thomasina, 72, 100
    Tomaxina, widow of
        Petrus, 376

Rosu
    Geço, daughter of
        Augustinus, of
        Venice, 701
Rota
    Chursaffa, daughter of
        Michalicus de la, 566
    Georgius de la, 2
    Henricus de la, 711
    Matheus de la, 2
    Michalicus de la, 566
Rubeis
    Pax, wife of Petrus de, of
        Padua, 64
    Petrus de, of Padua, 64
Ruberio
    Boiardis, Bonafacius de,
        comestabilis
        equester, 511
    Boiardis, Cinellus de, 512
Rubeus, 461
Rubin
    iudeus, 631
    Marcus, 568
    Richiolda, wife of
        Marcus, 568
Rubina
    Alexandro, de, 260
rubinum, 49, 94, 110, 195,
    234, 288, 640, 654
Rubri
    Iacobus, presbyter, cantor
        cretensis, 412
Rucadello
    Çorçi, 362
Rucha, 80
Ruçini, Rucino, Ruçino
    Aniça, 877
    ca', 548
    Helena, 57
    Iacobina, 699
    Marchesina, wife of
        Vasilius, 380
    Marco, 333
    Marcus, 703
    Marcus, de Venetiis, 877
    Marinus, 551
    Marinus, de Venetiis, 703

    Michael, 434, 437
    Nicoletus, clericus, 423
    Vasilius, 380
ruga
    Magistra, 274, 409, 424
    Porchorum, 121
Rugerachius, Ruzerachius
    Rugerio, de, 746
    Rugerio, de, son of
        Petrus, 158
Rugerio
    Constantinus de, 158
    Contessa, wife of Paulus
        de, 269, 592
    Dominicus de, 532, 569
    Francus de, 743
    Helena, daughter of
        Iohannes de, 569
    Hemanuel, 157
    Iohaninus, son of
        Constantinus de, 159
    Iohannes de, 157, 263,
        569
    Marcus de, 158
    Maria, wife of Iohannes
        de, 158, 569
    Paulus de, 145, 269, 569,
        592, 746
    Paulus, son of Iohannes
        de, 569
    Petrus de, 158, 263, 569,
        743, 745, 946
    Rageracius de, 951
    Rugerachius, son of
        Petrus de, 158
    Ruzerachius de, 746
    Salamona, wife of
        Francus de, 743
Rugerius, 269
    Georgius, 852
Ruigio
    Iacobus de, 738
Ruselena
    Soy, 669
Rusia
    vinea, 591
russa
    Maria, slave, 692

procuratores, 354
S. Margio, 329
S. Maria, 362, 336, 507, 710, 753
 ecclesia, 222, 320, 607, 887
 ecclesia, Amari, 538
 ecclesia, Baraterii, 222
 ecclesia, Calesiani, 329
 ecclesia, Candelor, de la, 634
 ecclesia, Castri, 542
 ecclesia Castri Themensis, 617
 ecclesia, Cheraialini, 306, 597
 ecclesia, Chruchosti, 870
 ecclesia, Coleliani, 595
 ecclesia, Conave, 488
 ecclesia, Eleusa, 591
 ecclesia fraternitatis de Sithia, 902
 ecclesia, Ialini, 599
 ecclesia, Macelo, 940, 992
 ecclesia, Manolitissa, 150, 597
 ecclesia, Mesochefala, 162
 ecclesia, Monomeritissa, 542
 ecclesia, Muctare, 542
 ecclesia, Nicolai Staniaro, 488
 ecclesia, Paço, 538
 ecclesia, Paliotissa, 878
 ecclesia, Paraschi, 313
 ecclesia, Pirgiotissa, 451
 ecclesia, Pirgo, 328
 ecclesia, Sinda, 823
 ecclesia, Spanopuliotissa, 482
 ecclesia, Valverde, 425, 638, 682, 746, 859, 928
 ecclesia, Varuchena, 486
 ecclesia, Vigli, 904
 ecclesia, Vlacheranitissa, 766
 fraternitas, 776, 789, 845
 guardianus scole, 656
 hospitale, 62, 320, 328, 315, 325, 328, 437, 776, 818, 826, 845, 994
 hospitale fraternitatis, 810
 hospitale mulierum, 887
 hospitale novum, 93, 83, 355, 888
 hospitale S. Spiritus, 96
 infirmi, 99, 428
 misse, 715
 monasterium, 370
 prevedhi et poveri, 83
 scola, 28, 62, 93, 96, 370, 420, 437, 826
 scola fraternitas Sithye, 975
S. Maria Angelorum
 ecclesia, 20, 148
S. Maria Anunciatio
 ecclesia, 793
S. Maria, burgo Castri Belvidere, 402
S. Maria Cruciferorum, 103, 172, 275, 465, 497, 552, 553, 566, 573, 927, 987
 conventus, 420
 ecclesia, 9, 20, 117, 154, 162, 182, 189, 190, 198, 225, 249, 266, 267, 270, 273, 324, 327, 337, 379, 434, 436, 437, 439, 452, 461, 469, 473, 482, 488, 505, 530, 611, 619, 629, 634, 641, 671, 682, 692, 700, 705, 714, 720, 722, 744, 746, 806, 810, 813, 816, 868, 875, 898, 906, 933
 fratalia, 45
 fraternitas, 724, 831
 guardianus, 441
 hospitale, 20, 158, 179, 187, 210, 233, 257, 259, 262, 267, 269, 270, 284, 286, 294, 296, 298, 302, 307, 417, 504, 562, 566, 634, 637, 645, 700, 705, 714, 722, 781
 hospitale novum, 53, 57, 68, 72-74, 76, 80, 86, 89, 91, 95, 107, 110, 332, 724
 hospitale novum vocatum Spiritus Sancti, 44
 hospitale vetus, 72, 76, 95, 347, 928
 infirmi, 35, 68, 81, 89, 184, 252, 332, 432, 424, 425, 489, 500, 505, 535, 603
 monasterium, 153, 233, 264, 332, 396, 519, 741, 742, 985
 monasterium ecclesie, 560, 567
 presbyteri, 93
 prior, 535
 sacerdotes, 302
 scola, 45, 53, 57, 68, 72, 73, 76, 80, 86, 89, 91, 95, 107, 110, 187, 218, 249, 271, 284, 286, 440, 664, 666, 667, 831, 880
S. Maria de Angelis
 ecclesia, 411
S. Maria Dei Genitrix
 ecclesia, 574
 hospitale, 720
S. Maria Dei Genitrix Panagia, 156
S. Maria Formosa contrata, 831
S. Maria Grecorum fratalia, 655
S. Maria Grogopacusa, 558
S. Maria dicta Gorgopaussa locus, 503
S. Maria Evançelistrea
 ecclesia, 347

S. Maria La Grande, 688
  prior, 866
S. Maria Magdalena, 103, 598,
  915, 930
  ecclesia, 30, 58, 90, 184,
    233, 242, 249, 256,
    261, 275, 294, 298,
    315, 700, 706, 829,
    838, 856, 901, 920,
    924, 927, 929, 974,
    991
  fraternitas, 968
  fratres, 187, 194
  monasterium, 96, 186,
    267, 296, 746, 859
  scola, 675
S. Maria Maior
  congregatio, 412
  ecclesia, 20, 26
  hospitale, 18, 23
S. Maria Malfatanis
  (Malfatanorum)
  ecclesia, 93, 345
  monaca ecclesie, 81
S. Maria Mater Domini
  ecclesia, 255
S. Maria Militum, de Militibus
  ecclesia, 20, 249, 461,
    619, 985
S. Maria Misericordia
  ecclesia of Venice, 68
S. Maria Odicitria
  ecclesia, 940
S. Maria Panagia
  ecclesia, 153
S. Maria, Rethimo, 994
S. Maria ton Anghelo
  ecclesia, 854
S. Maria Zubanigo
  contrata, 905
S. Marina
  ecclesia, 222
S. Michael, 452
  ecclesia, 18, 252, 417,
    965, 970, 983
S. Michael Archangelus
  ecclesia, 227, 543
  ecclesia maior, 218

S. Michael da ca' Faletro
  ecclesia, 698
S. Michael de Iesse
  ecclesia, 695
S. Michael de Vergici
  ecclesia, 849
S. Michael Magnus
  ecclesia, 327
S. Moyses de Venetiis
  confinium, 531
  contrata, 454
S. Nicolaus, 514
  ecclesia, 18, 103, 237,
    243, 284, 292, 327,
    417, 619, 816, 878,
    923, 970, 983
  ecclesia, a Molendinis,
    838
  ecclesia, apud Lunbium,
    154
  ecclesia, Chamaleuri, 672
  ecclesia, casale Calessia,
    345
  ecclesia, casale Mulia, 58
  ecclesia, Chanea, 457
  ecclesia, Soldino, 695
  ecclesia, Starcator maris
    austri, 603
  ecclesia, Vergiçi, tu, 794
  ecclesia, Veraidha, 19
  ecclesia, Vergici, 18, 278,
    680, 708, 775
  ecclesia, Verludha, 327
  monasterium, Calocorio,
    949
  Marino, Iacobus,
    presbyter, de
    Scaragatore, 402
S. Onufrius
  calogerus, 766
  monasterium, Pigadulia,
    306
S. Paliotissa, 288
S. Pantaleo, S. Pantaleon
  ecclesia, 19, 841
  monasterium, 621
  territorium, 420
S. Panthaleon

confinium, 830
S. Parasceva
  ecclesia, 163
S. Paraschi de Sophio
  ecclesia, 541
S. Paulus, 688
  ecclesia, 838, 858, 971
  Iohannes de, of Spoleto,
    540
  monasterium, 834
  prior, 859
  vinea, 99
S. Paulus Apostolus
  altar, 511
S. Perimbleto, 514
S. Petrus, 82, 325, 327, 362,
  370
  conventus, 722
  ecclesia, 89, 91, 93, 96,
    154, 182, 284, 294,
    327, 334, 344, 511,
    682, 687, 700, 806,
    857, 859, 950, 964
  frari, 896
  guardianus scole, 656
  monasterium, 230, 389,
    888, 962
  provencialis monasterii,
    704
  sorores, 182
S. Petrus de Castello
  confinium de Venetiis,
    756
S. Salvator, 125, 950
  conventus Heremitarum,
    875
  ecclesia, 402, 675, 682,
    683, 687, 692, 714,
    741, 806, 857, 862,
    868, 876, 880, 890,
    898
  ecclesia, Caloydhena, 538
  ecclesia, Chefala, 869
  ecclesia, Monomeriti, 315
  ecclesia, Salicichies, 542
  ecclesia, tu Saclichi, 874
  Fratres Remitani, 592
  monasterium, 389, 859,

896
Sabathea
iudea, 892
Sabba
Iohanina, 652
Sabella
Gulielmo, widow of
Iohannes, 402
Sabeta
Georgius, wife of
Rugerius, 852
Quirino, widow of
Marcus, 856
Sacerdos
Michael, iudeus, 127
Salachayas, iudeus, 170
S. Tito, 439, 442
Sachelari
Helena, 869
Iohannes, papas, 695
Sachielari
Georgius, papas, 533
Saclichi
Constantinus, 316
Georgius, called
Caçomata, 596
Helena, daughter of
Iohannes, 543
Hemanuel, papas, 874
Iohannes, 296, 543, 600
Maria, 296
Maria, widow of
Georgius, called
Caçomata, 596
papas, 240
Stephanus, 211, 297, 928
sachonum, 130
Sacreto, see Secreto
sacristia
S. Titus, 859
sagitarius
Nicolaus, 730
Sagitta
Costas, son of Nicolaus,
119
Michael, son of Nicolaus,
119
Nicolaus, 119

Saigata, 48
Salacaigas, Salacaya
iudeus, 127, 642, 650,
653
iudeus, sacerdos, 170
Salamon
Angelus, 583
Cethus, 121
Francisca, 551
iudeus, 809
Salamona
Stephanus, 643
Rugerio, wife of Francus
de, 743
Salamoneta, 487
Gradonico, widow of
Andreas, 415
Mocenigo, 154
Salamonus
Thomas, 318
Salera
Verona, daughter of
Palencius de, 438
Salivara
Hemanuel, 845
Salomica
Gradonico, widow of
Andreas, 259
Salomon
Curtesi, iudeus, 142
liber, 273
Marcus, 201, 727
Michael, 145
Salomono
Michael, 167
Petrus, naturalis, 607
Salonicha
Maria, slave, 240
Salonichea
Maria, 777
Salu
Andreas, 490
Salusia
Andreas, 531
Salusto
Iacomina, 397
Salvator Noster
ecclesia, 222

Samargias
Anguro, 579
Cumaro, iudeus, 821
Gavdhi, iudeus, 142
iudeus, 167, 608
Samaco
Franciscus, frater, 57
Sambatheus
Balbo, iudeus, 595
Casani, iudeus, 988
Chasuri, iudeus, 809
iudeus, 809, 821
Vlimichi, iudeus, 142
Samea
Calinichi, monaca, 181
Sameadena
Potha, 891
Samerya
Cali tu, iudea, 892
Rodo, de, iudeus, 892
Samuel
iudeus, 155
Nomico, iudeus, 123
San Francesco, see S.
Francisco
San Pier, see S. Petrus
San Salvador, see S. Salvator
San Zane de Torcello, 356
Sanbathus, see Sambatheus
Sancta Mater
ecclesia, 905
Sancti, Sanctis
Alexander, son of
Marcus, 544
Georgius, presbyter, 676,
932
Helena, calogrea,
daughter of Pasia,
415
Iohannes, 596
Marcus, 231, 544
Maria, 754
Marula, wife of
Thomasinus, 677
Pasia, 415
Petrus, 230, 543
Philipa, widow of Petrus,
230

Marula, 292
Marula, daughter of
  Paulus, 343
Michael, 292
Michael, preco, 783
Nicolaus, 722, 963, 969
Nicolaus, clericus, 242,
  494
Nicoletus, 866, 927
Nicoletus, clericus, 369
Paulus, 343, 927
Perardus, 843
Potha, wife of Iohannes,
  ex-slave, 779
Richiolda, wife of
  Iohannes, 284
Rosa, 18
Thomasina, 370
Turre, 285
Zanachius, 611
Segna
  Nicolaus de, 711
Segnolo
  Agnes, 224
  Caterina, 294
  Marcus, 147
  Maria, 294
segolum, 196
Segredo, see Secreto
seler
  Costas, of Constantinople,
    561
Selerno
  Guilielmos da, 540
Sella
  Petrus, 968
sellarius
  Çanbon, Marinus, frater
    scole S. Marie
    Cruciferorum, 441
Selopulena
  Cherana, 326
  Herini, 326
Selopulo
  casale, 132, 281
  Constantinus, 326
  Floreta, wife of Georgius,
    aurifex, 792

Georgius, 25, 670
Georgius, aurifex, 79,
  304, 792
Giorgici, calogerus, 982
Helena, wife of Georgius,
  670
Herini, daughter of
  Nicolaus, 26
Herini, wife of
  Moscoleus, 135
Iohannes, son of
  Georgius, aurifex,
  792
Maria, wife of Georgius,
  aurifex, 304
Michael, 575
Michali, 25
Moscaleus, 135, 670, 792
Moscalis, 25
Nicolaus, 25
Nicolaus, son of
  Georgius, aurifex,
  792
Stephanus, 25
Selu
  Maria, 724
Sen Gliguor, see S. Gregorius
Senda
  Alexander de, 58
Seni
  Brunelo, wife of Petrus,
    of Stimpalia, 12
Senis
  Franciscus de, magister,
    cirurgicus, 203
  Michael de, 867
serptelarii, 887
Serepeti
  Guillelmus, de Prinea,
    397
Serepeze
  Guillelmus, 456
  Marcus, 456
Serfioti
  Georgius, son of Michali,
    475
  Mariola, wife of Michali,
    475

Michali, 475
Sergius
  Venetando, 678, 816
  Villanus, 720
Serigo, Sirigo
  Georgius, 700
  Iohannes, 214, 228
  Iohannes, papas, 852
  Marcus, 948
  Moscoleus, 586
  Paraschra, 857
  Theodorus, 946
serva
  Efegenu, 39
serventaria, 885, 905
  Agia Maria, 210
  Aitania, 312
  Amari, 539
  Archanis, 671
  Cato Vathia, 159
  Cherassia, 86
  Chumeriaco, 629
  Cida, 369
  Embari, 969
  Fiugenichi, 125
  Gurnia, 262
  Larano, 478
  Larioma, 472
  Lembaro, 472
  Novo, 289
  Partira, 262
  Pendamodi, 258
  Passalite, 337
  Percinolicia, 812
  Pirgu, 157
  Polemissa, 268
  Riema, 969
  Russiochorio, 210
  Schylochorio, 211
  S. Iohannes Condu, 354
  Staurachi, 705
  Vadhipetro, 433
  Vathea, 369
serviciale, servicialis, 380
  Adrosi, daughter of
    Marcus, 826
  Cali, 116
  Calicia, 812

Iohannes, 589, 600, 604
Stadi, Stadhi
  Herini, 700
  Marcus, 572, 607
  Nicolaus, 528
  Petrus, 701, 721
Stadhiati
  Michael, called Mauro,
    564
Stadhiatissa
  Herini, 564
Stadioti
  Georgius, 899
  Maria, wife of Georgius,
    900
Stamarino
  Carentanus, 496
  Francisca, wife of
    Nicolaus of Venice,
    496
  Margarita, daughter of
    Nicolaus of Venice,
    496
  Nicolaus of Venice, 496
Stamario
  Iacobus, 496
Stamata, 854
  baiula, 905
  Conapioti, daughter of
    Dimitrius, 789
  Marcello, 716
  Prachimi, daughter of
    Georgius, fusarius,
    696
Stamati, 86
  Andreas de, 337
  Cadeneço, cimator, 477
  Chisamodi, son of Stratigi,
    953
  Goro, 75, 599
  Metupa, papas, 667
  papas, 802
  Portu, de, 370, 692
  slave, 614
  Tonello, 766
  Traversario, subdiaconus,
    414
  Xida, son of Xenus, 388

Stamatina
  Balastro, daughter of
    Franghia, 932
  Ranerio, wife of
    Anatalinus de, 628
Stamatini, 288, 426, 543, 792,
  902
  Achycli, wife of Leo, 665
  Gligoropula, 685
  iudea, 650
  Iustiniano, wife of
    Iohannes, 469
  Raguseo, daughter of
    Marinus, 502
  slave, 9, 57, 224, 287, 590
  Taiapetra, 224
  Taliapiera, 776
Stamatino
  Marinus, 649
Stamatinus
  Acheli, 647
  Costomiri, 303
  Davallerio, 708
  Mulida, villanus, son of
    Hemanuel, 927
Stamatius, 964
  Bellamore, de, 350
  Bono, 885, 890
  Çabela, 950
  clericus, 578
  Clugia, de, 537, 538, 541,
    545
  Dado, 134
  Goro, 142
  Gradonico, 752
  Langadhioti, 281
  Liveri, son of Georgius,
    corrigarius, 213
  Maçamano, son of
    Philipus, 206
  Metupa, 214
  Mudacio, 699, 955, 991
  Musgeta, 287
  Portu, de, 691, 881
  Quirino, 690, 845
  Scandalero, 880
  Trignan, 788
Stamius, 252

casale, 164, 214
  Iulianus de, 287
Stampa, 90, 443, 548
Stampalia, 39
  Constança de, 331
Stamurena
  Cartore, Audochia,
    called, 347
Stancharia
  Bonasudhus de, 400
  Iacobina, daughter of
    Manfredinus de,
    soldatus, 400
  Manfredinus de, soldatus,
    of Ferrara, 400
Stapsa, 330
Stathena, 195
Stathi
  Cali, 647
  Egidius, 914
  Nicolaus, 646
Statuta Venetiarum, 817
Stauracha
  locus, 388
Staurachena, 281
  Cali, 990
Staurachi, 374
  Agnes, 427
  Cali, 397
  Calicia, 395
  casale, 257, 705, 706
  Iohannes, 220, 685, 686
  Iohannes, presbyter, 381,
    918, 964
  Marcus, frater, 826
  Maria, 220
  Michael, 973
  Philipa, widow of
    Iohannes, 220
  serventaria, 705
Stauracho
  Iohannes, 218
Stauratum, 443
Stavris
  Herini, 614
Stecha
  Contareno, Marcus,
    called, 568

Lio, ex-slave, 621
Madalena, 391
Magdalena, wife of Petrus
    Bualli, 353
Marcus, 530
Marinus, 933
Marula, daughter of Petrus
    Bualli, 353
Matheus, 368, 586, 621,
    861, 911
Nicolaus, 65, 709
Nicolaus, notarius, 178
Nicolota, daughter of
    Petrus Bualli, 353
Petrus Bualli, 352, 388
Piero, 391
Potha, 852
Stamatini, 224, 776
Thomasina, natural
    daughter of Petrus
    Bualli, 354
Victor, 435, 586, 823
Zanachius, 368
Talypera, see Taliapetra
Taneligena
    calogrea, 542
Tanoligo
    Nicolaus, 564
Tanto
    Iohannes, 341
    Marchesina, widow of
        Marcus, 923
    Marcus, 264, 320, 923
tapetum, 29, 273, 354, 708,
    798
taputeum, 511
Taquista
    Nicolaus, 814
Tarachina
    Potha, 469
Tardina
    iudea, 595
Tarono
    Clara, daughter of
        Matheus, 756
    Graciolla, wife of
        Matheus, 756
    Matheus, de Venetiis, 756

tartara
    Margarita, slave, 759
    Maria, slave, 719, 720,
        727
    slave, 343
Tartaro, Tataro
    casale, 133
    Iohannes, marangonus,
        212
    Marmaia, Michael de, 287
    Mosco, Iohannes de, 287
tartarus
    Georgius, 473
    Georgius, slave, 982
    Gici, Georgius, slave, 975
    Iohannes, slave, 752
Tarte
    Costa, murarius, 770
tarvisanus
    Fosalta, Civeçel de, civis,
        398
Tarvisio
    Açonibus, Riçolinus de,
        de, comestabilis
        equester, 398
taulatum, see tabulatum
Tavian
    Quirin, 333
Tavigia
    iudeus, 650
tavladum, 79, 94
Tebaldo, 163
tebardum, 146
Tedaldo
    Angelus, 481
    Angelus, peliparius, 403
    Bartholomeus, 263
    Fragerius, 196
    Frugerius, 271
    Henglerosa, 195
    Iohannes, 263
    Petrus, 800
Tegmali
    castrum, 227
Tengo
    Florencia, de, 287
Teocari
    Angelus, 258

Helena, 298
Iacobina, 202
Iacobina, widow of
    Angelus, 258
teotonicus
    Ares, caporalis, 511
    Iacobus, iudeus, 738
    Ysacharus, iudeus, 935
Terfona
    locus, 388
Terra
    Andreas de, 444
    Andreas de, presbyter,
        822
    Dominicus de, 427
Terre
    Parlatus, 578
Tervisio
    Dominica, widow of
        Franciscus de, 78
    Franciscus de, 78
    Thomas de, 739
textrix
    Belena, 930
Thalasino
    Agnes, daughter of
        Iohannes, 604
    Dimitrius, 589, 604
    Herini, daughter of
        Iohannes, 590
    Herini, wife of Dimitrius,
        589
    Iohannes, 590, 604
    Maria, daughter of
        Iohannes, 604
    Michael, 979
    Nicoletus, son of
        Dimitrius, 590
Thedaldo
    Petrus, 673
Thefanu, Theffanu
    Matriera, 497
    monacha, 804
Themeni, Thamali, Themeli
    castrum, 191, 616
    Michael, 240

Theocaropulo, Thocaropulo
  Costa, called Ripus, 845
  Georgius, called Archavli,
    845
  Georgius, called Pothus,
    845
  Georgius, called Vircto,
    845
  Georgius, son of Costa,
    845
  Hemanuel, papas, 845
  Iohannes, called
    Servoiani, 845
  Micali, called Vilius, 845
  Petrofani, calogerus, 845
  Petrus, 845
  Theocarus, 845
Theocarus
  Thocaropulo, 845
Theocrepasto
  ecclesia, 769
Theodora, Theodoria,
    Thodora, 61, 125, 148,
    254, 325, 552, 669, 829
  Caçunu, 149
  Cacura, 968
  Cafato, wife of
    Constantinus, 221
  Castamoniti, daughter of
    Iohannes, 926
  Chera, 706
  Dato, wife of Adhamus,
    26
  Exeraquisti, tu, 788
  Facadena, bella, 826
  Faletro, de domu, 818
  Grassa, 184
  Langadioti, wife of
    Georgius, 922
  Maçamurdena, 824
  Macrimali, daughter of
    papas, 49
  Mamani, 475
  nena, 62, 257
  pauper mulier, 461
  Pillicena, 38
  Pisano, widow of
    Michael, 75

  Rodio, wife of Nichitas,
    181
  servitrix, 706
  slave, 86, 161, 185, 296,
    314, 556, 574, 603,
    686, 769, 786, 862,
    883, 979
  Suriano, wife of
    Vassilius, 51
  Venerio, 840
  Vergici, wife of Iohannes,
    520
Theodorellus, Thodorellus
  Geno, 374
  Venier, 710
Theodori
  Acladha, 804
Theodorus, Thodorus
  Achulo, de, 242
  Alimussi, 768
  blachus, 287
  bordonarius, 183
  Canali, de, 736
  Carpathio, 303
  Cauco, 302, 938
  Çavardalino, 245
  Clado, 894
  Condo, 517
  Contareno, 168
  Diminiti, 123
  Emforus, 173, 175, 176,
    178, 180, 182, 185,
    188, 191, 205, 226,
    238, 296
  faber, 578
  Franco, 132
  Gemisto, medicus, of
    Constantinople, 207,
    282
  Gisi, 286
  Grattaparte, 517
  Ialina, villanus, 507
  Lathura, 52
  Latura, son of Iohannes,
    674
  Maçamurdi, 966
  Masochopo, 516
  Mercato, 114

  Murtaro, 287
  Pandecho, son of
    Iohannes, 911
  Parasco, 806
  presbyter, 617
  Raça, 577
  Rapani, 640, 654
  Sclivi, papas, 832
  Scordili, 466
  Sirigo, 946
  slave, 264, 311, 542, 875
  Spano, bastasius, 680
  Speçalinça, 66
Theodosius
  Armachi, 310
  aurifex, 614
Theodoti
  nena, 35
Theodulli
  calogrea, 806
Theofillus
  confessor SS
    Apostolorum, 47
  Costas, 614
Theofilopulo
  Maria, calogrea, 689
Theologa, Theologu, 312
Theologiti, 810
  Aniça, 119
  Dimitrius, cerdo, 119
  Gradonico, wife of
    Iohannes, preco, 375
  Moscana, nena, 838
Theologo
  Cherarini, 713
  Georgius de, papas, 310
Theolosia
  Gradonico, wife of
    Nicolaus, 856
Theophanu
  ancila, 154
Theostictus
  Bono, penitencialis, 784
Theostineus
  calogerus, pneumaticus,
    708
  confessor SS
    Apostolorum, 947,

Tonello
  Andreas, 524
  Frangula, wife of Stamati, 766
  Michael, 525
  Stamati, 766
Toneuco
  N., 565
Tonfeo
  Nicolaus, 440
Tonina
  slave, 121
Tonisto
  Andreas, 754
  Iacobus, 951
  Iohannes, 938
  Nicolaus, 117, 118, 122, 124, 126, 129, 131
  Petrus, 696
  Thomasina, soror, 498
Tor
  Veneranda de la, 924
Torcello
  Angelinus de, 980
  Georgius de, 98, 980
  Hemanuel, called Bonfadio, 118
  Herini, 118
  Iohannes de, 98, 327, 578, 769
  Iohannes de, natural son of Simon, 98
  Iohannes de, notarius, 69, 98
  moniales of S. Iohannes, 454
  Nicolaus de, frater, provincialis Fratrum Predicatorum, 98
  Pasquale, F., de, 385
  Pasqualigo de, 702
  Pasqualis de, 355
  Philipa, daughter of Georgius, 98
  Raphael, preco, 588
  Simon de, 97, 98
  Thomas de, 98, 578
Tore

Marchesina de la, 869
Philipus de la, 113
Torello
  Andreas, 893
  Georgius, 893
  Herini, daughter of Petrus, 212
  Mariçoli, wife of Andreas, 893
  Minoti, 893
  Nicolaus, 205
  Petrus, 212
Tornari
  Caterina tu, 869
Tornichio
  Cali, widow of Michael, papas, 769
  Michael, papas, 769
Tosa
  slave, 264
Toscano
  Elena, daughter of Maria, 443
  Bonacursius, 299
  Maria, 443
  Micaletus, subdiaconus, 429
  Michael, 423
  Michael, presbyter, 442
tovagia, 78
tovalia, 183
Trachanioti
  Hemanuel, 156, 602
Trano
  Nicolo, 866
Trapano
  Cola de, equestatorus, 739
traponta, 183, 262, 706, 781, 974
Traversario, 429, 818
  Andreas, 637
  Andreas, barberus, 686
  Angelus, 869
  Aniça, 508
  Benedictus, 339
  Bentivegna, notarius, 639
  Çanachius, 921

Dominica, 685
Dominicus, 197
Dominicus, subdiaconus, 427
Franciscus, 849
Iacobus, 656
Iohannes, 676, 693, 956
Iohannes, clericus, 429
Iohannes, presbyter, 179, 578
Iordanus, 588
Marcus, 427, 508, 509
Maria, 419
Nicolota, 325
Petrus, 637
Sançoni, presbyter, 95, 686, 693, 909, 923
Stamati, subdiaconus, 414
Thomasina, 811
Tredentino
  Nicolaus, 266
Tredento
  Fredericus de, magister, fisicus, 25
Trentino
  Bartholomeus, 472
Trento
  Antonius de, 989
  Margarita, widow of Antonius de, 989
Trepes, 773
Triandafilo
  Agnes, widow of Iohannes, papas, 253
  Herini, widow of Nicolaus, 253
  Iohannes, papas, 253
  Nicolaus, 253
Tricha, 632
  Calicia, daughter of Iani, papas, 591
  Georgius, 141, 580, 598
  Georgius, son of Iani, papas, 591
  Herini, wife of Iani, papas, 590
  Iani, papas, 590

Nicolaus, natural son of
Fucha, 539
Vasilius, 539
Vanno, Vano
Angelus de, 217
Helena, wife of Angelus
de, 217
Nicolaus de, frater, 26
Vaqua
Gulielmus, 677
Iacomina, daughter of
Gulielmus, 677
Varangus
Morgano, 485
Varda
Calergi, 337, 507
Vardali
Georgius, 328
Maria, wife of Georgius,
329
Vardalina
Maria, de Calessia, 98
Vardhena
Maria, 466
Vareta
Marinelus, 849
Vari
Georgius, 138
Varillu
Herini, 811
varnacia, 883
varnaconum, 375
Varnavas
Geromonacus,
penitencialis, 778
varnimenta, 9, 98
varnitura botonorum, 754
Varsalu
Moscana, 466
Varsama
Hemanuel, villanus, 202
Truno, wife of Donatus,
671
Varucha
Costas, 506
Varuchenena
Maria, 316
Varucha

Helena, chira, nena, 826
Varvara
slave, 964
Varvari
casale, 20, 224
Peroni, Nichiforus, papas,
564
Vasili, 603
Crasudhi, 77
Petronicola, 533, 574
villanus, 517
Vasilico
Gregorius, 697
Vasilinus, 697
Vasilicus
Vasilino, 697
Vasilii
Agnes, 746
Vasilius, 29, 39, 76
Andrinopoliti, papas, 984
Calona, 29
Carasa, 122
Carofilaco, 311
Pinaca, 968
Vanichi, 538
Vasilu, 601
Vasmuli, Vasmulo
Christina, tu Carandino,
856
Maria, wife of Nicolaus,
534
Magistropiero, Marinus,
called, 516
Nicolaus, 533
Vassalo, Vaxallo
Agnes, daugther of
Marcus, 875
Agnes, widow of
Iohannes, 619
Alexander, 20, 620
Andreas, 20, 620, 682,
875
Andreas, sutor, 682
Antonius, 213
Georgius, 195, 620, 720,
875
Helena, 418
Herini, 327

Iacobellus, 703
Iacobellus, son of
Marcus, 875
Iacobina, daughter of
Georgius, 620
Iacobinus, 764
Iohannes, 21, 619, 875
Iulianus, 20, 327, 619,
838, 875
Marchesina, 875
Marcus, 21, 37, 213, 327,
357, 359, 360, 875
Marcus, scriba palatii,
339, 341
Maria, 620, 716
Maria, daughter of
Iulianus, 20
Maria, natural daughter
of Andreas, 620
Maria, widow of
Riçardus, 422
Marcioli, 465
Nicolaus, 283, 930
Ota, 682
Palma, widow of
Georgius, 195
Petrus, 53, 391, 418, 683,
720, 831
Petrus, clericus, 940
Riçardus, 422
Vaxilius, 262
Veneranda, 866
Zanachi, natural son of
Alexander, 620
Zanachius, 875
Vassilichi
Maria, 94
Vassilius, Vassilus
Iustiniano, 381
Peroni, 564
Rucino, 380
Suriano, 51
Vastarchi, see Vestarchi
Vataçi, Vataci
Andreas, 150
Eudochia, wife of
Michael, 150
Georgius, 134

Iohannes, 110
Mariçoli, 890, 909, 972
Mariçoli, wife of
  Nicolaus, 190
Marinus, 327, 630
Marinus, de contrata S.
  Thodorie, 338
Marula, 395, 709, 716,
  811, 974
Matheus, 275, 279
Michael, 466
Nicolaus, 49, 110, 190,
  225, 463, 527, 890
Nicolaus maior, 235
Nicoleta, 812
Nicoletus, 93, 812
Nicolota, wife of
  Bartholomeus, 195
Nida, daughter of Piero,
  710
Nida, natural daughter of
  Dominicus, 818
Ninda, widow of Petrus,
  425, 452, 817
Paulus, son of Maria, 429
Petrus, 164, 225, 235,
  284, 425, 452, 536,
  551, 635, 811, 817
Petrus, son of Frangulius,
  225
Philipa, 81
Philipa, widow of
  Frangulus, 422
Piero, 710
Polo, 336
Riço, 338
Theodora, 840
Thodorello, 710
Thomas, 169, 225
Thomasina, daughter of
  Iohannes, 110
Titus, 235, 679, 994
Zan, 338
Venerio Grata
  Biriola, 266
Venetanda
  caligaria, 380
  piçocara, 814

Venetando
  Albani, daughter of
    Iohannes, 105
  Angelina, 104
  Angelus, frater, 93, 627
  Aniça, wife of Nicolaus,
    papas, 192
  Antonius, son of
    Hemanuel, 816
  Cherana, 669
  Christina, wife of
    Hemanuel, 816
  Dominicus, 627, 669
  Hemanuel, 337, 453, 816
  Heregina, wife of
    Nicolaus, 337
  Iacobus, 863
  Iohannes, 70, 104, 198,
    643, 816
  Leonardus, 41, 43, 627
  Marchesina, 248, 693
  Marçoli, daughter of
    Hemanuel, 816
  Maria, wife of Iohannes,
    104
  Micheleta, 925
  Michaleta, wife of
    Iohannes, 198
  N., 627
  Nicolaus, 269, 337, 678,
    816
  Nicolaus, called Pubana,
    208
  Nicolaus, papas, 192
  Petrus, 626
  Regina, wife of Nicolaus,
    678
  Rosa, mother of Iohannes,
    105
  Sergius, 678, 816
  Viola, widow of Petrus,
    626
Venetiae
  Marçoli, 404
Venetian
  Aniça, 109
  Niça, 931
Venetiano

Franciscus, 902
Marula, wife of
  Franciscus, 902
Nicolaus, 169
Venetiarum
  Nicolaus, diaconus, 420
Venetiis
  Donatus de, presbyter,
    940
Venetus
  Cauco, Georgius,
    presbyter, cantor
    ecclesie Crete, 858
Veni
  casale, 222
Venice, 82, 202, 210, 242,
  260, 275, 314, 334, 354,
  359, 370, 398, 457, 495,
  528, 659, 661, 671, 698,
  700, 703, 714, 734, 743,
  747, 756,
  Baldu, Fantinus, 897
  Barbadico, Nicolaus, 721
  Bernardus, Paulus de,
    740
  Bertazanus de, 400
  Bolan, Franciscus, 843
  Bono, Alexander, 897
  Cabriel, Çacharia, 914
  Çafredo, Thomasinus,
    781
  Çane, Philipus, 254
  Castelana de, 265
  Çeno, Iohannes, 410
  Contareno, Franciscus,
    567
  Contareno, Marinus,
    called Barbadusia,
    335
  Contarini, Thomas, 410
  Coppo, Iohannes, 914
  Çordano, Iohannes de,
    coraçanus, 935
  Cornario, Andreas, 265
  Cornario, Iohannes, 364
  Cornario, Petrus, 741
  Çote, Nicoletus, 409
  Dandulo, Gratonus, 958